A BRIEF EXPLORATION OF THE

Hebrew Bible/Old Testament

A BRIEF EXPLORATION OF THE

Hebrew Bible/Old Testament

Theodore Burgh

University of North Carolina—Wilmington

cognella®
SAN DIEGO

Bassim Hamadeh, CEO and Publisher
David Miano, Senior Specialist Acquisitions Editor
Michelle Piehl, Senior Project Editor
Jeanine Rees, Production Editor
Jess Estrella, Senior Graphic Designer
Stephanie Kohl, Licensing Coordinator
Natalie Piccotti, Director of Marketing
Kassie Graves, Vice President of Editorial
Jamie Giganti, Director of Academic Publishing

9781516575084

cognella® | ACADEMIC PUBLISHING
3970 Sorrento Valley Blvd., Ste. 500, San Diego, CA 92121

Contents

Chapter VIII: Late Monarchic Period   125

Chapter IX: Wisdom Literature   137

Index   141

Detailed Contents

Preface

This work developed from my teaching an Introduction to the Hebrew Bible/Old Testament for a number of years. Many of the questions and ideas I had as a child fuel my desire to engage students in their quest for knowledge. Moreover, my experience and discussions with students have helped to develop ideas, thoughts, and questions to effectively present this subject in the classroom. For many students, my course is their first in religion. At times their backgrounds are diverse. Some come from religious households or religious-centered institutions. Others have no religious affiliation at all and have never studied the Bible. To be an effective instructor, I have to learn how to present the material in a way that is engaging, challenging, intriguing, and not dogmatic.

A Brief Exploration of the Hebrew Bible/Old Testament effectively introduces to the student necessary material in stages and portions that are not overwhelming. The book is designed for students to read before the lecture. The work will enhance and amplify essential aspects of the Bible and other ancient texts and different ideas and methodologies. Pictures and photographs also contribute to illuminating and illustrating various points.

CHAPTER 1

Introduction: Hebrew Bible/ Old Testament

Introduction

Growing up, I knew that my grandmother worked as a maid for two elderly Jewish sisters. I didn't know what being Jewish meant, so this term didn't make much of an impact on me. It was just another adjective. However, one odd thing about the sisters that stood out to me was my grandmother telling us that they had two sets of dishes—yes, dishes. She told us the ladies had china they used every day, but they also had specific dishes for holidays and special Jewish occasions. My grandmother described how she had to wash and store the exclusive vessels and platters in a designated cabinet, and they had to be handled with care. I didn't understand everything she shared, but I knew that these dishes were extraordinary and linked to events that were meaningful to these women. These artifacts were an essential aspect of their culture and religious practices. Our family had special dishes too, but they weren't anything like this.

My grandmother never uttered anything derogatory about the women, their cultural practices, or Judaism. I know that she thought that some of their actions were a little different compared to how she lived, but she respected their beliefs and practices. I also remember her talking to my father about the unique, beautifully crafted letters printed on some of the dishes. I inquired what they were, and he explained that they were Hebrew. That was even more baffling. What in the world was Hebrew? He shared that Hebrew was a language used by Jews. To help me better understand, he added that it was the language in which the Old Testament was written. I still didn't quite get it, but I knew the language and letters were connected to the dishes and the sisters' religious practices.

In addition to my grandmother and father discussing the sisters and their dishes, I heard people at school talking about certain folks being Jewish. These conversations didn't have a significant effect on my life then. I innocently viewed "Jewish" as something people were and knew there were certain requirements. It wasn't until college that I learned more about Judaism. For instance, it was then that I first encountered the term *Hebrew Bible*. This appellation had never been a part of my world or in my vocabulary. I thought the Bible was the Bible. I vaguely understood what the Hebrew language was and its connection with the biblical text. Where I lived, I didn't hear any Hebrew words, at least none that I recognized. I didn't know the letters or what they represented. I heard that Jewish people celebrated many holidays, and that there were certain things they didn't or couldn't do during these times. But their cultural practices never really came up in the midst of my childhood playing and learning. My grandmother and father's conversations didn't reveal much, but their dialogue planted a seed. Little did I realize that I would revisit these memories many years later in my academic pursuits.

The Purpose of This Book

Why this book? I have designed this book to give a very brief but solid introduction to students interested in the Hebrew Bible/Old Testament and the world from which it comes. I encourage students and readers to continue their study in additional passages and books not covered here. It is my hope that this overview will spark the desire to learn and study more.

My innocent ignorance sparked a desire to know more about the Hebrew Bible/Old Testament, its peoples and cultures, where and how they lived, and their languages. I wanted to hear more than ill-informed diatribes and rhetoric based on misquoted ancient passages. Thankfully, I have had plenty of opportunities to address these desires. Along the way, I have gleaned insightful methods of pedagogy and inspiring educational approaches from some of the best scholars in the world. Thus, I have designed this book both for those who have never opened a Bible and for those who have experience with the text. I have done this by using various critiques and readings and by incorporating, comparing, and contrasting other ancient Near Eastern writings; the study of known peoples and cultures of the ancient Near East; archaeological artifacts; theories and methods from other disciplines, such as anthropology, history, and art; and personal experience.

Another goal of this work is to provide a glimpse into the wonderful, enigmatic world of the ancient Near East in general, and Israel in particular; provide a solid foundation that will assist in further biblical study; and challenge students to think critically about antiquity, diverse peoples, and cultures we continue to work to understand.

The information in the following pages, the corresponding course lectures, and the variety of assignments will challenge and teach the reader or student to always, always ask questions. Never be afraid to inquire. Don't be afraid to use the gray matter between your ears and think. You may not find every answer you seek, but you may actually learn something new about the world of the ancient Near East and yourself.

How to Use This Work

Keep in mind that this textbook is a very brief introduction. There will be subjects, topics, and materials that will be familiar to some; however, there will also be ideas, aspects of texts, and other information that many have never seen before. Some of it will be easy to understand and digest. Other portions may present different kinds of difficulties. Nevertheless, keep an open mind and think critically about everything encountered. As you proceed in life, you will encounter copious amounts of information. The challenge is to figure out what will be accepted, questioned, or investigated and how it will be used. This book, coupled with the class, will provide very usable tools to do this.

Note that all translations are from the New Revised Standard Version or generated by the author unless otherwise indicated.

1. Why do you want to study the Hebrew Bible/Old Testament? Please dig deeper than "It is a required course"!
2. What do you expect to learn from introduction to Hebrew Bible/Old Testament?
3. What do you think you bring to this course?

CHAPTER 2

Archaeology of Ancient Israel

I'M SURE MANY of you have heard about Indiana Jones or seen at least one of the movies. If you haven't, you should. The films are highly entertaining and definitely worth viewing. How can you not enjoy seeing an archaeologist outrunning an enormous, rolling boulder; skillfully maneuvering his way out of a pit of venomous, hissing, slithering snakes; successfully outwitting conniving villains; or finding priceless, powerful artifacts and taking them out of the country of origin without issue? It's enjoyable, wonderful, entertaining cinema, but many of the actions are highly questionable when it comes to understanding what archaeologists actually do.

As enjoyable as Dr. Jones and his adventures are, it is important to note that he never really excavates anything. The closest he comes is when he unscientifically determines a particular area is "the spot" and dramatically tells workers to "Dig here." *Lara Croft:, Tomb Raider*, the gun-toting, acrobatic, and brilliant archaeologist brought to life by Angelina Jolie, is also entertaining, but one has to always be mindful that this is fantasy. It's exhilarating to watch Ms. Croft skillfully ride a motorcycle

FIG. 2.1 **Raiders of the Lost Ark**

on a narrow stone wall, dodge bullets sprayed from machine guns, and battle ancient stone warrior statures. However, these engaging events have no real connection with archaeology and the study of the ancient world.

I am an archaeologist. I've spent many seasons in the field, but I've never been chased by a huge stone, fallen into a pit full of snakes, run from villains, or attempted to take priceless artifacts out of a country without requesting permission. If I had done the latter, I would probably have written this book from a prison cell. As exciting as all of those things appear, archaeology doesn't work that way. Adventures like these are hardly typical. I've seen a snake or two, but they were quickly trying to get out of our way. Local residents often inquire about excavations taking place in their backyards, and every now and then the discussions can be tense, but they are hardly villains. If anything, local residents have helped to shed light on the history of the area and enlightened us regarding intricate cultural customs.

I've had the distinct pleasure of working in Israel, Jordan, and Sicily, and it's always breathtaking to see the remains of past worlds and societies. It's even more exhilarating to witness artifacts emerging from the dirt pregnant with valuable information about the peoples and cultures from which they come. Archaeology is a rich, vital contributor to understanding the world of the Hebrew Bible/Old Testament.

What Is Archaeology?

Whether we realize it or not, we've all participated in archaeology in some form or fashion. Searching through trash for items or digging in one's own backyard—these are forms of archaeological excavation. We would be hard pressed to find a continent where archaeology has not or is not taking place. Very simply, archaeology is the study of the past through the analysis of material culture.

The ground holds history and data that cannot be found in texts. Artifacts and the area in which they are found are important. Their presence leaves clues in the earth. Thus, "reading the dirt" is an essential element in helping to understand what has transpired. This information gives insight regarding how people have engaged in and navigated their surroundings.

Furthermore, the terrain, climate, and geographical location, among other factors, determine how excavations take place. For example, approaches to excavations in rainy climates with deciduous and coniferous vegetation and muddy soil will differ from those in arid areas. Archaeologists also continue to develop techniques to excavate under water. The discipline has the unique ability to provide incredible perspectives into the cultures and peoples of the past.

What Do We Call It?

A brief perusal of archaeological literature connected to the Hebrew Bible/Old Testament shows that there are several names for archaeology in this part of the world. They include but are not limited to the following:

- Archaeology of Ancient Israel
- Biblical Archaeology
- Near Eastern Archaeology
- Syro-Palestinian Archaeology
- Middle Eastern Archaeology
- Middle East Archaeology

This book employs primarily the terms *Near Eastern Archaeology* and *Syro-Palestinian Archaeology*, as these are more in line with the geographical region. Moreover, the term *Biblical Archaeology* often narrows the field and produces labels and other issues that are not helpful and can create unnecessary tensions; not every aspect of excavation in this area involves the biblical text.

Geography of Ancient Israel

Israel is a fractured landscape. In other words, the terrain, climate, and fauna differ as one moves through the country. In the far north, the terrain is lush and verdant and even contains hot springs and other bodies of water (e.g., the Sea of Galilee). Moving south, the land becomes more arid, increases in rocky terrain and mountain ranges, and eventually comes into the barren region of the Negev Desert. To designate the way the terrain changes across the country, Israel is often divided into six zones. Each has specific and distinct characteristics of soil, climate, and population.

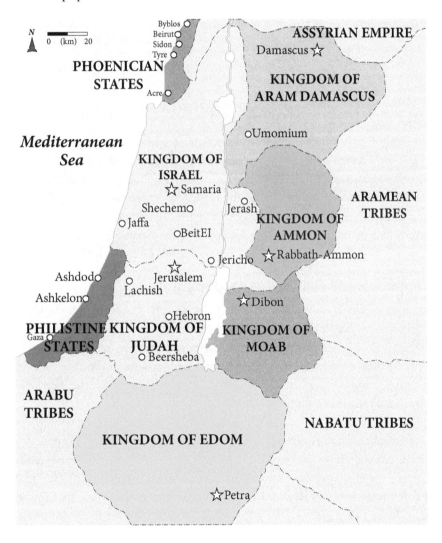

FIG. 2.2 Geographical Map of Ancient Israel

Zone 1	**Coastal or Maritime Plain**. Coastal areas, beaches.
Zone 2	**Shephelah or Low Foothills**. Most crops raised here, vegetation grows well; most populated area.
Zone 3	**Central Hills**. Similar to the Shephelah, but starts to become more arid, with rocky terrain.
Zone 4	**Jordan Rift Valley**. Rocky, mountainous terrain, arid; contains the Dead Sea, Sea of Galilee, and Jordan River.
Zone 5	**Transjordan**. Arid, with light vegetation for sheep and goat herds.
Zone 6	**Desert**. Vast, extremely arid; some groups, such as the Bedouin, spend time here.

Africa and Israel

Many biblical stories have intricate connections with the continent of Africa, especially the country of Egypt. In the context of the ancient Near East, Egyptians are often involved in battles with other superpowers, such as the Assyrians or Babylonians. Africa in general, and Egypt in particular, are integral components of this part of the world. It is important to recognize connections between Israel and Africa. In addition to Egypt, Israel has interactions with Ethiopia, the African country often identified as the Horn of Africa and the biblical land of Cush (Nubia or Sudan), and Libya, which was biblically identified as Put (Gen. 10:6; 1 Chron. 1:8).

Some Peoples of the Ancient Near East

A plethora of peoples lived all over the Near East in antiquity. Many are well known; others are limited to the pages of ancient texts and remain enigmatic (e.g., Girgashites, Japheltites, Perrizites, etc.). Scholars continue to seek information and material from these little-known groups. In the meantime, archaeological excavations and textual studies reveal much about many other ancient peoples and their cultures. Following are brief descriptions of some of those who are more well known and are encountered in the Hebrew Bible/Old Testament.

Egyptians. This magnificent group was one of the major superpowers of the ancient Near East. Their power ebbed and flowed for centuries, but Egyptian influence is constantly visible in areas such as material culture, language, and architecture in surrounding cultures. The Egyptian chronological time periods that cross with the biblical period of Israel, or Late Bronze and Iron Ages (1500–586 BCE) are the New Kingdom Period (ca. 1580–1069 BCE; 18th–20th Dynasties), the Third Intermediate Period (ca. 1069–715 BCE; 21st–25th Dynasties), and the Late Period (ca. 715–332 BCE). There were many rulers/pharaohs reigning during this time. Some of

AFRICA

FIG. 2.3 Map of Africa and Ancient Israel

the most popular known during this time (the biblical period) include those depicted in the following figures:

FIG. 2.4 Queen Hatshepsut (1498–1483 BCE)

FIG. 2.5 Amenhotep IV, a.k.a. Akhenaten (1350–1334 BCE)

FIG. 2.6 Sphinx of Taharqa (690–664 BCE)

FIG. 2.7 Egyptian Goddess Bastet

FIG. 2.8 Merneptah (1212–1202 BCE)

FIG. 2.9 Ramesses II (1279–1213 BCE)

Other prominent pharaohs with links to Israel include Sheshonq I, a.k.a. Shishak (945–924 BCE), and Shabaka (716–702 BCE). With the possible exception of Akhenaten, the Egyptians practiced forms of polytheism and henotheism. Polytheism was ubiquitous in ancient Near Eastern cultures. Popular deities in Egypt appear in Israel and influence surrounding cultures: Amun/Amen (sun god), Bastet (goddess of warfare), Hathor (sky goddess), Osiris (god of the afterlife), and numerous others. Henotheism is the worship of a specific chief deity while still paying homage to others. The Egyptians may have briefly also practiced monotheism under Akhenaten.

The geographical region inhabited by this people is known by many names: Egypt (from the Greek *Aegyptos*, which came from the pronunciation of the Egyptian name Hwt-Ka-Ptah, meaning "Mansion of the Spirit of Ptah"), Kemet (Black Land), "the Land of the Riverbank" (referring to the Nile), and Misr (meaning "country"). It is also important to remember that Egyptians are Africans.

Assyrians. This group was another dominant superpower of the ancient Near East. The chronological time period that intersects with the biblical period of Israel is the Neo-Assyrian (ca. 883–609 BCE). Like the Egyptians, Assyrians were polytheistic for the most part, and their influence is visible in surrounding culture and languages. Known deities include Marduk, Tiamat, Tammuz, Shamash, Ishtar, Anshar, and Sin. Notable Assyrian kings include Ashurnasirpal, Asurnirari, Shalmaneser, and Tiglath-Pileser.

FIG. 2.10 **Tiglath-Pileser III (745–727 BCE)**

FIG. 2.11 **Shalmaneser III (859–824 BCE)**

FIG. 2.12 Ancient Relief of Assyrians Fighting

FIG. 2.13 Representation of the Goddess Ishtar

Babylonians. This group rounds out the trio of the ancient Near Eastern superpowers. The chronological time span that crosses with the biblical period of Israel is the Neo-Babylonian period (ca. 625–539 BCE). The Babylonians were also polytheistic overall, and many Assyrian deities were also a part of the Babylon pantheon and other Near Eastern groups, although the names of these deities may vary by language. Known gods in the Babylonian pantheon include Marduk, Tiamat, Ea, Damkina, Kishar, and Shamash. Nabopolasser (658–605 BCE) was a notable king of Babylon. He is often credited with founding the Neo-Babylonian period. However, the most well-known Babylonian king is Nebuchadnezzar, the infamous antagonist of the biblical Daniel story.

FIG. 2.14 Marduk

Hittites. This is one of the most enigmatic groups of the ancient Near East. The primary reason is that it is uncertain what happened to them. Most groups diminish in number as their zenith declines; their material cultural remains appear less frequently in the archaeological record, and those members of the group still remaining are often absorbed into surrounding cultures and communities. But with the Hittites, they simply and abruptly disappear. They aren't absorbed into other groups. Their material cultural remains stop abruptly—they're just gone. The chronological time period that crosses with the biblical period of Israel are the Late Bronze and Iron Ages (ca. 1700–1200 BCE). The Hittites were also polytheistic. While they were never a superpower, they often took the Egyptians to task, and although the Hittites could never overtake them, they won several battles. Known Hittite deities include Apaliunas, Hannahannah, and Inara.

Canaanites. This group was one of many that lived in the land known as Canaan, which eventually became Israel. This group was also polytheistic, with known deities such as Baal, El, Asherah, Astarte, and Anat. What is unique about the Canaanites is that they have a special relationship with Israelites. The two peoples are practically identical. Although the biblical text presents the Canaanites as villains and drastically different from the Israelites, from a material culture standpoint, it is almost impossible to tell them apart. Moreover, the Canaanites and Israelites occupied the same geographical area.

Israelites. The biblical writers consistently focus on this group and their development. Like the previous peoples, the Israelites were polytheistic and also contained elements of henotheism and monotheism. Known deities include many that were part of the Canaanite pantheon: El, Yahweh, Baal, and others. At one point, Asherah and Yahweh were consorts (i.e., husband and wife).

FIG. 2.15 Hittite lionesses flanking Hittite city

FIG. 2.16 Canaanite Fertility Figurines

FIG. 2.17 A possible representation of the Canaanite/Israelite Goddess Asherah from Tel Rehov

Chronology in Ancient Israel

Understanding time periods in antiquity is another essential aspect of studying the Hebrew Bible/Old Testament. Long before the exciting chronologies described in the biblical text, Israel was populated with various cultures, even in the prehistoric period. The working chronology for ancient Israel that encompass the biblical period discussed in this course are as follows:

Period	Dates	Events of Note
Middle Bronze Age I (MB I) (Early Bronze Age IV)	2300–2000 BCE	First Intermediate Period in Egypt
Middle Bronze Age IIA (MB IIA)	2000–1750 BCE	Old Assyrian and Old Babylonian Periods
Middle Bronze Age IIB (MB IIB)	1750–1550 BCE	Hyksos in Egypt
Late Bronze Age	1550–1200 BCE	New Kingdom in Egypt
Iron Age	1200–1000 BCE	Exodus; Period of the Judges
Iron Age IA	1000–925 BCE	Assyrian Invasion; Demise of Israel
Iron Age IIB-C	925–586 BCE	Babylonian Invasion; Demise of Judah
Iron Age III	586–539 BCE	Introduction of the Persian Period

What Is a Tell?

The ancient Near East is remarkable in that it contains *tells*. Only a few places in the world have this incredible phenomenon. These man-made hills develop through various peoples' occupying the same living space over centuries. Some tells may display a one-period human occupation, while others may show centuries of peoples existing continuously or at various intervals in the area. People often used remains of the previous occupants' dwellings, built on top of them, and expanded the living area. As a result of this practice, layers of occupation accumulated, creating large mounds. These hills possess and display a timeline of occupation of the site, along with debris such as pottery, foodstuff, and other archaeological remains literally frozen in time. Outside of Israel (Mexico, Ohio, Illinois, etc.), similar mounds often serve as burial or ceremonial structures, which is different from the mounds in the ancient Near East.

FIG. 2.18 **View of Beth Shean**

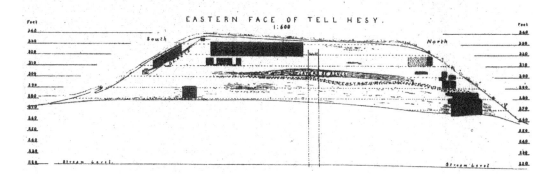

FIG. 2.19 **Cross section of a tell**

Some Basic Archaeological/Material Cultural Terminology

Stratigraphy: The analysis of the order and position of layers of archaeological remains; the structure of a particular set of strata or layers.

Artifact: An object, often made by humans, typically of cultural or historical interest.

Baulk: A ridge left unplowed between furrows. Baulks are created as excavators remove dirt and debris from an archaeological site.

Carbon-14 Dating: The process of using a long-lived, naturally occurring radioactive carbon isotope of mass 14 to determine the age of an object, also used as a tracer in biochemistry.

A Few Words About Languages and Associated Terminology

Excavations often produce texts that must be translated. Some of the languages that were used in the ancient Near East include but are not limited to Akkadian, Aramaic, Egyptian hieroglyphs, Hebrew, and Sumerian. The earliest writing systems of the ancient Near East helped produce and disseminate these languages. Following are some essential terms and examples connected to ancient

FIG. 2.20 **Cuneiform Writing**

FIG. 2.21 **Egyptian Hieroglyphs**

Near Eastern languages (note that Akkadian, Sumerian, and others use the cuneiform writing systems):

Pictograph: A pictorial symbol for a word or phrase. Pictographs were used as the earliest known form of writing; examples have been discovered in Egypt and Mesopotamia from before 3000 BCE.

Cuneiform: Denoting or relating to the wedge-shaped characters used in the ancient writing systems of Mesopotamia, Persia, and Ugarit, surviving mainly impressed on clay tablets (see example in Fig. 2.20).

Lexicon: A dictionary, especially of Hebrew, Aramaic, Syriac, or other ancient languages that shows spellings, etymologies, cognates, and uses of words and phrases.

Excavating a tell and other ancient Near Eastern sites produces artifacts and other data that assist in better understanding how peoples of the past lived, interacted with each other, and navigated the land.

STUDY QUESTIONS

1. How do you think archaeology assists in helping understand the past?
2. How can one employ archaeology and ancient texts together to study past cultures and peoples?

Formation of the Hebrew Canon

Canon

What is a canon? When it comes to the Hebrew Bible/Old Testament, a canon is essentially a collection or list of books that are accepted by communities as sacred or special. Interpretations of these works often govern how certain groups or individuals live their lives, interact with others, and understand the world in which they live. The 39 books of the Hebrew Bible/Old Testament are part of a canon.

Textual Criticism

There are no original manuscripts of the Hebrew Bible. We cannot go to the "original source." Scholars must study the ancient biblical texts (e.g., scrolls, codices) that have survived over time. The pool of available sources continues as new discoveries are shared.

All of the texts and textual fragments scholars employ are handwritten and in the original biblical languages (Hebrew, Aramaic, and Greek). Scholars study them, make comparisons between them, and even conduct comparative work with writings in other Near Eastern languages, such as Akkadian, Egyptian, Hittite, Phoenician, as well as others. This approach helps scholars to comprehend issues such as misspelled or previously untranslatable Hebrew words. This method can generate an eclectic text (a text in which several variants are used to establish the best translation, e.g., New Revised Standard Version, New International Version).

Various Critical Approaches to Studying the Biblical Text

There are many ways to enter the text to extract valuable information and generate insightful viewpoints. These perspectives are known as critiques or criticisms. Often when we hear or read these terms, they usually conjure images of derogatory reviews and analyses, but they are much more than that. In this instance, a critique is an analysis of the text from a specific perspective, with carefully crafted queries, theories, and ideas. We will explore a few of these briefly.

Narrative Criticism

This type of critique explores areas such as the writer's original intent, how the narrative or plot is put together, how and why the author(s) may have chosen certain words, and how all of this connects to a main theme. In essence, it's a historical kind of approach to studying the text. This is not practiced as much as it once was.

Historical Criticism

This approach studies the text in conjunction with events that may have been contemporary with what is written. For example, if the writers mention a specific king, study of his reign and activities connected with it may shed insight. This critique also employs archaeology and history.

Form Criticism

Form criticism attempts to determine the original form of each portion of the narrative and the reason it was eventually set in its final form. Typically, form criticisms will make comparisons between different versions of the same episode or narrative piece (e.g., the Ten Commandments in Exod. 20:1–17 and the laws listed in Exod. 34:17–26).

Redaction Criticism

This critique works to understand the editing or redactions that have taken place in the text. In other words, one using redaction criticism would examine matters such as anachronisms (things not in sequential or chronological order) and references to outside material/sources.

Canonical Criticism

In this approach, there is an interest in the final form of the text within the larger context of the entire biblical text. One of the most important issues is exploring questions regarding how the text is used to address the faith concerns of the community that uses it. Here the books of the Bible are not viewed as individual texts or passages but as part of an overall story.

Social-Scientific Criticism

This criticism involves the use of tools (theory and method) from the social sciences (psychology, anthropology, sociology, etc.) to understand the biblical world and many of its practices. For instance, one may incorporate anthropological methodology in order to study areas such as ritual and cult, kinship, or family structure.

Feminist Criticism

The feminist criticism attempts to examine the importance of women in the ancient world and how they influence the shaping of the culture, as well as the biblical narrative.

Womanist Approach

This criticism attempts to employ the social construction of black womanhood and the black community in connection with the biblical narrative.

Reader Response Criticism

This approach assumes that there is a relationship between sender, message, and receiver, whether the reader is a concrete person or only a hypothetical one. In this criticism, the reader has the ability to decode and understand what is in the text.

Rhetorical Criticism

The goal of this criticism is to describe the ideology that is embedded in the text in order to see how its very construction has preconditioned the experience for both the writer and the reader.

Traditional Criticism

This approach is concerned with the community or group responsible for the shaping and transmission of a particular text. Another important element is the geographical location with which a tradition is associated.

Following is the most well-known academic criticism.

Documentary Hypothesis or Source Criticism

The Documentary Hypothesis or Source Criticism method is a theory or idea to explain the construction of the Pentateuch (the first five books of the Bible: Genesis, Exodus, Leviticus, Numbers, and Deuteronomy) and possibly other portions of the biblical text.

Briefly, during the Enlightenment Period (17th–18th centuries CE), people began to present perplexing questions regarding the biblical text. These queries derived from close readings of many biblical stories:

- *Why are there different names for the Israelite deity?*
- *Why is there replication/duplication of stories?*
- *Why are there different names for the same character in the same story?*
- *Why are there variations in language and style?*

Although other scholars were involved in addressing these inquiries and concerns, Julius Wellhausen is often credited with the development of Source Criticism or the Documentary Hypothesis. This theory states that the Pentateuch and later books were developed by four authors or editors. They are identified as "J," "E," "D," and "P."

General Characteristics of the Documentary Hypothesis

J source (*The Yahwistic Source*): This source likely developed around 900 BCE, possibly in the south, or Judah. (The geographical region of Israel was eventually divided into Israel [North] and Judah [South]; this division will be discussed in more detail later.) In the J source, the deity speaks directly with people in anthropomorphic (human characteristic) fashion. The deity, often referred to as LORD (Yahweh, or Yahweh), is very immanent—in the realm of reality, close. J-source material dominates the patriarchal narrative (that of Abraham, Isaac, and Jacob).

E source (*The Elohistic Source*): This source generally dates to the mid-ninth century, around 850 BCE, and is thought to have originated in the northern kingdom of Israel. The deity is often referred to as God (Elohim). In this source, the deity tends to speak with people through dreams and visions. Moses is "the man" in the E source and held the example of righteousness par excellence. The E source dominates the Exodus material.

D source (*The Deuteronomistic Source*): This narrative, which is more than likely simply a redaction of the J and E sources plus additional sources, was a product of King Josiah's reformation in 622 BCE. The purpose of the reformation is to persuade the people to abandon their local cultic sites in favor of a centralized cult in Jerusalem. Those responsible for this change had a hand in producing the Deuteronomistic History (i.e., the books of Joshua, Judges, Samuel, and Kings). This history also promotes the idea of a centralized religion or cult. A synopsis of the D source is as follows:

- Worship Yahweh only
- Worship Yahweh according to the priests
- Worship Yahweh only in Jerusalem

P source (*Priestly source*): This narrative is concerned with cultic (i.e., sacrificial, ritual), genealogical, and other types of details. There is a concentrated effort to give a systematic account of the origin of all of Israel's cultic institutions. There has been some debate regarding the P source and dating this source. One school of thought is that it is the product of the Exilic period of Israelite history (i.e., the Babylonian Captivity). Another view is that the source has a long history, with many parts of it being as old as any of the Pentateuch, if not in some cases older.

STUDY/DISCUSSION QUESTIONS

1. How do you think archaeology and biblical studies can work together?
2. Which geographical zone would you prefer to live in? Why?
3. Do you think the Documentary Hypothesis is valid? Explain why or why not.

Credits

Fig. 2.15: Copyright © Carole Raddato (CC BY-SA 2.0) at https://commons.wikimedia.org/wiki/File:The_Lion_Gate_flanked_by_two_towers,_located_at_the_southwest_of_the_city,_the_lions_were_put_at_the_entrance_of_the_city_to_ward_off_evil,_Hattusa,_capital_of_the_Hittite_Empire_(25725048044).jpg.

Fig. 2.16: Copyright © Wellcome Images (CC by 4.0) at https://commons.wikimedia.org/wiki/File:Ancient_Canaanite_Teraphim._Figurines_of_fertility_goddess._Wellcome_M0008439.jpg.

Fig. 2.17: Copyright © Oren Rozen (CC BY-SA 4.0) at https://commons.wikimedia.org/wiki/File:Tel_Rehov_Exhibition_090316_06.jpg.

Fig. 2.18: Copyright © Israel BeitShean2 tango7174 (CC BY-SA 4.0) at https://commons.wikimedia.org/wiki/File:Beit_Shean_Wikivoyage.png.

Fig. 2.19: Source: https://commons.wikimedia.org/wiki/File:Flinders_Petrie_-_Tell_Hesy_-_Cross_section_through_the_mound.jpg.

Fig. 2.20: Source: https://commons.wikimedia.org/wiki/File:Sumerian_account_of_silver_for_the_govenor_(background_removed).png.

Fig. 2.21: Source: https://commons.wikimedia.org/wiki/File:Bm-epic-g.jpg.

CHAPTER 3

What is the Pentateuch?

THE PENTATEUCH (*PENTA*, "five"; *teuchos*, "books") consists of the first five books of the Hebrew Bible/Old Testament. These are the same books that make up the Torah, or the first section of the Tanak. It may also be referred to as the Books of Moses, a term found in Ezra, Nehemiah, and Chronicles. Most scholars concur that the Pentateuch is a composite of works that reflects several traditions, sources, and contributions. Essentially, more than one person is responsible for contributions to these books.

Some of the primary themes of the Pentateuch include the following:

Creation Stories. In most cultures ancient and modern, there are always questions regarding the origin of the universe, how and why humans and animals were created, and what is their purpose. Like that of nearly every group, Israelite culture contained stories that explored etiologies regarding how the world came to be, humans' place in it, and humans' complex relationship to a deity or deities.

Moses. There are often key figures in a group's culture who are integral to its development. In Israelite culture, this figure is Moses. He enters the biblical text in the midst of a genocide and miraculously survives and thrives. Moses is the central character of most of the Pentateuch. Over time, he becomes the major, almost superhero-like figure of Israelite history and culture. His rise begins during the Exodus story. Once the Israelites escape from bondage in Egypt, Moses, along with others, is vital in shaping the society, relationships, and lineages described by biblical writers in various stories and situations.

Exodus. Led by Moses, the Hebrews, or Israelites, escape Egyptian oppression and persecution. Once they make their momentous escape from Egypt, the group begins an adventure-filled trek to a land promised to their ancestors.

Becoming Israel. The Pentateuch also explains how the Israelites and their culture develop. Writers share intricate details regarding aspects of the development of Israelite beliefs and cultic institutions.

TABLE 3.1 Genesis

Priestly Creation Story	Gen. 1:1–2:4a
Yahwistic Creation Story	Gen. 2:4b–3:24
Story of Cain and Abel, birth of Seth and Enos	Gen. 4:1–26
Genealogy, age, and math of patriarchs from Adam to Noah	Gen. 5:3–21
Problems with humankind on the earth, selection of Noah, flood story, curse of Canaan	Gen. 6:1–9:29
Tower of Babel, generations of Shem, introduction of Abram	Gen. 11:1–32
Adventures of Abram (Abraham) and Sarai (Sarah)	Gen. 12:1–25:34
Stories of Isaac, Rebekah, Esau, and Jacob	Gen. 26:1–28:9
Adventures of Jacob	Gen. 30:25–35:29
Adventures of Joseph	Gen. 37:1–48:22
Jacob blesses his sons, mourning for Jacob	Gen. 49:1–50:26

Following are brief overviews of the books of the Pentateuch.

The word *genesis* means "origin" or "beginning"; it is the first book of the Pentateuch and introduces the cosmology of Israel. Genesis consists of basically two parts:

Primeval History. Focus is on all of humanity. This part of Genesis history discusses matters including a) the creation of the cosmos or universe and the first humans, presenting their relationship to the deity or deities and their place in the world, and b) the flood, why it happens, and the fate of the people after the flood.

Ancestral History. Focus is on Abraham, the other patriarchs, and their descendants. Ancestral history picks up where primeval history leaves off and tells the story of how the deity chooses Abraham and makes promises to him. The writers also introduce the 12 sons or tribes of Israel. Genesis also contains lists of descendants, which explain who descended from whom and who is related to whom and how.

Genesis also employs several literary motifs that appear throughout the Hebrew Bible/Old Testament:

The *barren motif.* A theme in which a woman is unable to bear a child; however, she often eventually does miraculously, and the child produced is often special (e.g., births of Isaac, Samson).

The *wife-sister motif.* A theme in which a husband has his wife pretend to be his sister in order to save his life and deceive a ruler (e.g., Abram and Sarai).

The *trickster motif*. A theme in which a character tricks another to achieve a goal or obtain an object of their desire. This character can also end up being tricked.

According to the Documentary Hypothesis (discussed in chapter 2), Genesis contains elements of the Priestly, Yahwistic, and Elohistic sources. For example, the creation stories that open Genesis are from the Priestly and Jahwistic sources, respectively.

Exodus is concerned primarily with the liberation of Israel from Egypt by the God of the patriarchs—Abraham, Isaac, and Jacob—a theme that originated in Genesis. This book also discusses Hebrew captivity, maltreatment, and suffering, in addition to describing events that led to the Israelites' liberation from oppression. Moses, the eventual leader of the Israelites, has a special birth (though not originating from a barren

FIG. 3.1 **The Tower of Babel. Pieter Bruegel the Elder**

motif) through which he escapes Hebrew genocide and rises to prominence within the palace of the Pharaoh. Moreover, the book contains an explanation of several laws, which attempt to distinguishes Israel's culture and its people, and instruction for construction of the tabernacle.

TABLE 3.2 Exodus

Birth of Moses	Exod. 1:1–2:10
Moses in Midian	Exod. 2:11–4:17
Genealogy	Exod. 6:13–27
Plagues and the Origin of Passover	Exod. 6:28–12:30
Exodus from Egypt	Exod. 12:31–13:16
Crossing the Red Sea/Sea of Reeds	Exod. 13:17–15:21
Mount Sinai	Exod. 15:22–18:27
Ten Commandments	Exod. 19:1–20:21
Laws from Yahweh	Exod. 20:22–24:18
The Tabernacle	Exod. 25:31
Golden Calf Incident	Exod. 32:1–33:6
Tent Meeting	Exod. 33:7–23
The New Tablets	Exod. 34
Completion of the Tabernacle	Exod. 35:40

With the exception of the biblical story, it is important to note that there is no recorded evidence of an exodus or similar event in any ancient Near Eastern texts. Although there are no other texts or artifacts that discuss this event specifically, the Hebrew Bible/Old Testament writers place the Exodus in the sixteenth or fifteenth century BCE, or Late Bronze Age (1500–1200 BCE):

> *In the four hundred eightieth year after the Israelite came out*
> *of the land of Egypt, in the fourth year of Solomon's reign over*
> *Israel, in the month of Ziv, which is the second month, he began*
> *to build the house of Yahweh (1 Kgs 6:1).*

The lack of material support or archaeological data, other chronological issues, and the dominance of Egyptian culture during this time make dating the event using this passage highly problematic. Moreover, anecdotal stories that describe Hebrew slaves making bricks for pyramids are also inaccurate. If this somehow were the case, these stories would be anachronistic; the Exodus event must necessarily have taken place well after the construction of pyramids. Again, there are no extrabiblical texts that shed any light on an exodus or any slavery during this period.

There are two possibilities of who was the Egyptian pharaoh at the time of the Exodus. Pharaoh Seti I has been said to have been in power during the time of Exodus, but most scholars concur that it was in fact Ramesses II (ca. 1300–1250 BCE).

The writers introduce Moses to a world in which the Egyptian king, Pharaoh, is xenophobic. His fear of the Hebrews is so dire that he implements genocide—midwives are to kill Hebrew boys as soon as they are born. With the help of his mother and sister, the midwives, and Pharaoh's daughter's attendant, Moses survives this dangerous situation, and readers follow him into the Pharaoh's house. We are able to observe his connections to the royal family, his committing murder and fleeing to Midian, and his encounter with Yahweh, which changes the course of his life. Finally, Exodus makes a shift at chapter 20, as Moses shares with the people specific ordinances and statutes that will govern them and help shape their culture. Chapters 20–40 appear to contain elements of the P source. Aspects of the P source are in the earlier chapters, but they also contain parts of J and P.

FIG. 3.2 **Departure of the Israelites**

TABLE 3.3 Leviticus

Various Sacrifices	Lev. 1:1–17
Priestly System	Lev. 8:1–10:20
Regarding Purity	Lev. 11:1–17:6
Morality	18:1–27:34

The name of the book is associated with the Levites, a group of priests who came from the tribe of Levi. They were charged with handling priestly matters (e.g., attending to the Ark of the Covenant). Leviticus focuses on matters regarding the worship of God at the tabernacle during the Israelites' wilderness journey. Writings from the Priestly source material make up the entire book of Leviticus. As Wellhausen's Documentary Hypothesis indicates, the writings from Leviticus are straight to the point and focus on facts, instructions, and descriptions. Leviticus also shares information on matters such as various types of sacrifices and ceremonies, as well as moral and ethical laws that are a part of Israelite culture.

TABLE 3.4 Numbers

Israel in the Wilderness	Num. 1:1–22:1
Israel turns away from her deity	Num. 22:1–25:18
Reorganization of Israel	Num. 26:1–36:12
Commandments and Judgments	Num. 36:13

The name refers to the censuses that occur in the book. Numbers has three primary sections: a) preparations for wilderness travel, containing a census, the camp arrangement of the Israelites, and consecration of the Levites; b) travels in the wilderness, including rebellions and complaints by Israelites, Miriam, Aaron, and the scouts; c) the end of the wilderness travels, containing preparations for entering the land of Canaan and another census. Moses transfers civil leadership to Joshua just before they enter the land of Canaan.

FIG. 3.3 **Wilderness of Canaan**

TABLE 3.5 Deuteronomy

First Address of Moses	Deut. 1:1–4:49
Second Address of Moses	Deut. 5:1–26:19
Third Address of Moses	Deut. 27:1–34:12

The name derives from the Greek word meaning "second law." In this book, Moses on the eve of his death gives three speeches that have been grouped together as a lengthy valedictory address in which he a) reviews Israel's history to remind them from whence they come and how they should behave, b) discusses their laws and how they will be governed, and c) instructs them about the importance of loyalty to their god. Just before Moses goes the way of all flesh, he makes Joshua Israel's new leader. Joshua becomes the new Moses and will direct them into the land promised to their ancestors.

It appears that this text most likely developed in the seventh century BCE. It has elements of and is probably connected to Josiah's reformation during this same time period (622 BCE). With this reformation, Josiah pushed to centralize the Israelite religion and cult to Jerusalem, have the priests govern these practices, and make all focus on Yahweh. The reformation draws from previous practices and can be encompassed in a three-line mantra:

- Worship Yahweh and Yahweh only
- Worship Yahweh according to the priests
- Worship Yahweh only in Jerusalem

We will discuss Josiah's reformation in more detail in chapter 8.

Credits

Fig. 3.1: Source: https://commons.wikimedia.org/wiki/File:Pieter_Bruegel_the_Elder_-_The_Tower_of_Babel_(Rotterdam)_-_Google_Art_Project.jpg.
Fig. 3.2: Source: https://commons.wikimedia.org/wiki/File:David_Roberts-IsraelitesLeavingEgypt_1828.jpg.
Fig. 3.3: Copyright © Godot13 (CC BY-SA 4.0) at https://commons.wikimedia.org/wiki/File:Israel-2013-Ein_Avdat_02.jpg.

CHAPTER 4

Creation and Flood Myths of the Ancient Near East

Creation and Flood Myths

Myths are ubiquitous. They are often entertaining, insightful stories that attempt to explain the origin of something, someone, or a particular event. It is often difficult to determine where myths began or when and how they developed. Yet myths often become staples of groups and cultures.

There are several possible purposes of myths. These unique stories attempt to explain or shed light on matters that are complex or inexplicable (cf. etiology). In our own families and communities, there are stories that are passed along orally from generation to generation about senior family members' colossal accomplishments, neighborhood athletes' superhuman abilities, or once-in-a-lifetime phenomenal events. Some of these myths become an indelible part of family histories and communities. This was the case in antiquity. Most ancient cultures have creation stories or some explanation of the origin of the cosmos, the earth, and human beings. The interpretation of events and creation of myths help to shape cultural identity and define who they are.

Defining Myth

What is a myth? Defining this term (*muthos* [Greek], *mythus* [Modern Latin]) continues to be a subject of debate among scholars. The major issue is that traditional interpretations render definitions of myth as a false story, fabrication, or false belief or idea. However, a stronger, more adequate definition is a traditional story, especially one concerning the early history of a people or explaining some natural or social phenomenon, and typically involving supernatural beings or events. When studying and attempting to understand the ancient world, there are often misconceptions about what a myth is and its purpose within the culture. It should be understood, however, that myths are much more than fables or fairy tales. While they are not necessarily meant to explain events through tangible facts or scientific data, they often serve as essential etiological explanations that help to understand how peoples and cultures interpreted and navigated the world in which they lived.

The Genesis creation myths function in this manner. It is not a coincidence that they open the biblical text. Although the two stories are different in a number of ways, both share perspectives of the power and abilities of the Israelite deity, the place of humans in the cosmos, and humans' relationship to the animals, the earth, and the deity or deities.

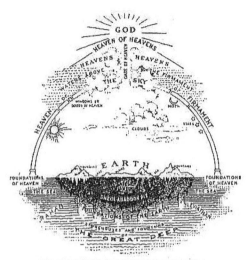

**THE ANCIENT HEBREW CONCEPTION
OF THE UNIVERSE**
TO ILLUSTRATE THE ACCOUNT OF CREATION AND THE FLOOD

Illustration from George L. Robinson, *Leaders of Israel*
(New York: NY: Association Press, 1913), p. 2.

Reprinted with permission from A.J. Mattill: The Seven Mighty Blows to
Traditional Beliefs, by A.J. Mattill. : Flatwoods Free Press, 1995.*

FIG. 4.1 **The ancient Hebrew conception of the universe**

The Genesis stories are identified as the Priestly and Jahwistic versions. The Priestly version (P) is found in Gen. 1:1–2:4a; the Jahwistic version (J) comprises Gen. 2:4b–11:31.

The Priestly Version in Genesis 1:1–2:4a.

Note the characteristics of Wellhausen's P source description from the Documentary Hypothesis. Can you identify the characteristics after nothing them?

[1] In the beginning when God created the heavens and the earth, [2]the earth was a formless void and darkness covered the face of the deep, while a wind from God* swept over the face of the waters. [3]Then God said, "Let there be light"; and there was light. [4]And God saw that the light was good; and God separated the light from the darkness. [5]God called the light Day, and the darkness he called Night. And there was evening and there was morning, the first day.

[6]And God said, "Let there be a dome in the midst of the waters, and let it separate the waters from the waters." [7]So God made the dome and separated the waters that were under the dome from the waters that were above the dome. And it was so. [8]God called the dome Sky. And there was evening and there was morning, the second day.

[9]And God said, "Let the waters under the sky be gathered together into one place, and let the dry land appear." And it was so. [10]God called the dry land Earth, and the waters that were gathered together he called Seas. And God saw that it was good. [11]Then God said, "Let the earth put forth vegetation: plants yielding seed, and fruit trees of every kind on earth that bear fruit with the seed in it." And it was so. [12]The earth brought forth vegetation: plants yielding seed of every kind, and trees of every kind bearing fruit with the seed in it. And God saw that it was good. [13]And there was evening and there was morning, the third day.

[14]And God said, "Let there be lights in the dome of the sky to separate the day from the night; and let them be for signs and for seasons and for days and years, [15]and let them be lights in the dome of the sky to give light upon the earth." And it was so. [16]God made the two great lights—the greater light to rule the day and the lesser light to rule the night—and the stars. [17]God set them in the dome of the sky to give light upon the earth, [18]to rule over the day and over the night, and to separate the light from the darkness. And God saw that it was good. [19]And there was evening and there was morning, the fourth day.

[20]And God said, "Let the waters bring forth swarms of living creatures, and let birds fly above the earth across the dome of the sky." [21]So God created the great sea monsters and every living creature that moves, of every kind, with which the waters swarm, and every winged bird of every kind. And God saw that it was good. [22]God blessed them, saying, "Be fruitful and multiply and fill the waters in the seas, and let birds multiply on the earth." [23]And there was evening and there was morning, the fifth day.

²⁴ And God said, "Let the earth bring forth living creatures of every kind: cattle and creeping things and wild animals of the earth of every kind." And it was so. ²⁵God made the wild animals of the earth of every kind, and the cattle of every kind, and everything that creeps upon the ground of every kind. And God saw that it was good.

²⁶ Then God said, "Let us make humankind* in our image, according to our likeness; and let them have dominion over the fish of the sea, and over the birds of the air, and over the cattle, and over all the wild animals of the earth,* and over every creeping thing that creeps upon the earth."

²⁷ So God created humankind* in his image, in the image of God he created them;* male and female he created them.

²⁸ God blessed them, and God said to them, "Be fruitful and multiply, and fill the earth and subdue it; and have dominion over the fish of the sea and over the birds of the air and over every living thing that moves upon the earth." ²⁹God said, "See, I have given you every plant yielding seed that is upon the face of all the earth, and every tree with seed in its fruit; you shall have them for food. ³⁰And to every beast of the earth, and to every bird of the air, and to everything that creeps on the earth, everything that has the breath of life, I have given every green plant for food." And it was so. ³¹God saw everything that he had made, and indeed, it was very good. And there was evening and there was morning, the sixth day.

Yahwistic Version in Genesis Chapter 2:4a–3:24.

Can you identify the characteristics of the J source in the second Genesis story?

⁴ In the day that the LORD God made the earth and the heavens, ⁵when no plant of the field was yet in the earth and no herb of the field had yet sprung up—for the LORD God had not caused it to rain upon the earth, and there was no one to till the ground; ⁶but a stream would rise from the earth, and water the whole face of the ground—⁷then the LORD God formed man from the dust of the ground, and breathed into his nostrils the breath of life; and the man became a living being. ⁸And the LORD God planted a garden in Eden, in the east; and there he put the man whom he had formed. ⁹Out of the ground the LORD God made to grow every tree that is pleasant to the sight and good for food, the tree of life also in the midst of the garden, and the tree of the knowledge of good and evil.

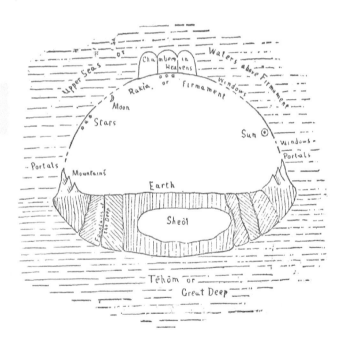

FIG. 4.2 **Another concept of Hebrew cosmology**

¹⁰ A river flows out of Eden to water the garden, and from there it divides and becomes four branches. ¹¹The name of the first is Pishon; it is the one that flows around the whole land of Havilah, where there is gold; ¹²and the gold of that land is good; bdellium and onyx stone are there. ¹³The name of the second river is Gihon; it is the one that flows

around the whole land of Cush. ¹⁴The name of the third river is Tigris, which flows east of Assyria. And the fourth river is the Euphrates.

¹⁵The LORD God took the man and put him in the garden of Eden to till it and keep it. ¹⁶And the LORD God commanded the man, "You may freely eat of every tree of the garden; ¹⁷but of the tree of the knowledge of good and evil you shall not eat, for in the day that you eat of it you shall die."

¹⁸Then the LORD God said, "It is not good that the man should be alone; I will make him a helper as his partner." ¹⁹So out of the ground the LORD God formed every animal of the field and every bird of the air, and brought them to the man to see what he would call them; and whatever the man called every living creature, that was its name. ²⁰The man gave names to all cattle, and to the birds of the air, and to every animal of the field; but for the man there was not found a helper as his partner. ²¹So the LORD God caused a deep sleep to fall upon the man, and he slept; then he took one of his ribs and closed up its place with flesh. ²²And the rib that the LORD God had taken from the man he made into a woman and brought her to the man.

Enuma Elish

An exciting creation story also appears in the Mesopotamian epic, *Enuma Elish*, also known as *When on High* or the *Epic of Creation*. Seven tablets discovered by Austen Layard and his team in 1849 and published by George Smith in 1876 present an action-packed story involving numerous male and female deities. There are Assyrian and Babylonian versions dating as early as 1500 BCE (Late Bronze Age). Some versions, such as the one from Ashurbanipal library may date to the seventh century BCE.

The story is an intricate epic that begins by tracing the relationships between gods and goddesses and their problems with contempt, envy, revenge, and murder. In tablet three, the battle begins between Tiamat and Marduk, two of the main characters. This eventually leads to the creation of the heavens and earth, along with human beings.

As one reads both the Genesis myths and the *Epic of Creation*, it is clear that the Mesopotamian writer and editors attempt to explain why and how the universe was created and human beings' place in it. Each of the Near East creation stories appears to respond to questions such as these: Where did we come from? Who made this place? What is our place in it? A popular perspective is that the J version of Genesis is a continuation of the P version. However, this is not the case; although a surface reading of the text gives the impression that the story is a continuation with more detail, close study reveals that the J version differs in many ways from the P version. Creation in the *Enuma Elish* is part of a much larger story and describes a process in making the land, humankind, and all else that is in contrast to both the Genesis stories.

Enuma Elish

Tablet I

1. When the heavens above did not exist,
2. And earth beneath had not come into being—
3. There was Apsû, the first in order, their begetter,

"Enuma Elish, Tablets I–VII," trans. Joshua J. Mark. Copyright © 2018 by Ancient History Encyclopedia Limited. Reprinted with permission.

4. And demiurge Tia-mat, who gave birth to them all;

5. They had mingled their waters together

6. Before meadow-land had coalesced and reed-bed was to be found—

7. When not one of the gods had been formed

8. Or had come into being, when no destinies had been decreed,

9. The gods were created within them:

10. Lah(mu and Lah(amu were formed and came into being.

11. While they grew and increased in stature

12. Anšar and Kišar, who excelled them, were created.

13. They prolonged their days, they multiplied their years.

14. Anu, their son, could rival his fathers.

15. Anu, the son, equalled Anšar,

16. And Anu begat Nudimmud, his own equal.

17. Nudimmud was the champion among his fathers:

18. Profoundly discerning, wise, of robust strength;

19. Very much stronger than his father's begetter, Anšar

20. He had no rival among the gods, his brothers.

21. The divine brothers came together,

22. Their clamor got loud, throwing Tia-mat into a turmoil.

23. They jarred the nerves of Tia-mat,

24. And by their dancing they spread alarm in Anduruna.

25. Apsû did not diminish their clamor,

26. And Tia-mat was silent when confronted with them.

27. Their conduct was displeasing to her,

28. Yet though their behavior was not good, she wished to spare them.

29. Thereupon Apsû, the begetter of the great gods,

30. Called Mummu, his vizier, and addressed him,

31. "Vizier Mummu, who gratifies my pleasure,

32. Come, let us go to Tia-mat!"

33. They went and sat, facing Tia-mat,

34. As they conferred about the gods, their sons.

35. Apsû opened his mouth

36. And addressed Tia-mat

37. "Their behavior has become displeasing to me

38. And I cannot rest in the day-time or sleep at night.

39. I will destroy and break up their way of life

40. That silence may reign and we may sleep."

41. When Tia-mat heard this

42. She raged and cried out to her spouse,

43. She cried in distress, fuming within herself,

44. She grieved over the (plotted) evil,

45. "How can we destroy what we have given birth to?

46. Though their behavior causes distress, let us tighten discipline graciously."

47. Mummu spoke up with counsel for Apsû—

48. (As from) a rebellious vizier was the counsel of his Mummu—

49. "Destroy, my father, that lawless way of life,

50. That you may rest in the day-time and sleep by night!"

51. Apsû was pleased with him, his face beamed

52. Because he had plotted evil against the gods, his sons.

53. Mummu put his arms around Apsû's neck,

54. He sat on his knees kissing him.

55. What they plotted in their gathering

56. Was reported to the gods, their sons.

57. The gods heard it and were frantic.

58. They were overcome with silence and sat quietly.

59. Ea, who excels in knowledge, the skilled and learned,

60. Ea, who knows everything, perceived their tricks.

61. He fashioned it and made it to be all-embracing,

62. He executed it skillfully as supreme—his pure incantation.

63. He recited it and set it on the waters,

64. He poured sleep upon him as he was slumbering deeply.

65. He put Apsû to slumber as he poured out sleep,

66. And Mummu, the counsellor, was breathless with agitation.

67. He split (Apsû's) sinews, ripped off his crown,

68. Carried away his aura and put it on himself.

69. He bound Apsû and killed him;

70. Mummu he confined and handled roughly.

71. He set his dwelling upon Apsû,

72. And laid hold on Mummu, keeping the nose-rope in his hand.

73. After Ea had bound and slain his enemies,

74. Had achieved victory over his foes,

75. He rested quietly in his chamber,

76. He called it Apsû, whose shrines he appointed.

77. Then he founded his living-quarters within it,

78. And Ea and Damkina, his wife, sat in splendor.

79. In the chamber of the destinies, the room of the archetypes,

80. The wisest of the wise, the sage of the gods, Be-l was conceived.

81. In Apsû was Marduk born,

82. In pure Apsû was Marduk born.

83. Ea his father begat him,

84. Damkina his mother bore him.
85. He sucked the breasts of goddesses,
86. A nurse reared him and filled him with terror.
87. His figure was well developed, the glance of his eyes was dazzling,
88. His growth was manly, he was mighty from the beginning.
89. Anu, his father's begetter, saw him,
90. He exulted and smiled; his heart filled with joy.
91. Anu rendered him perfect: his divinity was remarkable,
92. And he became very lofty, excelling them in his attributes.
93. His members were incomprehensibly wonderful,
94. Incapable of being grasped with the mind, hard even to look on.
95. Four were his eyes, four his ears,
96. Flame shot forth as he moved his lips.
97. His four ears grew large,
98. And his eyes likewise took in everything.
99. His figure was lofty and superior in comparison with the gods,
100. His limbs were surpassing, his nature was superior.
101. "Mari-utu, Mari-utu,
102. The Son, the Sun-god, the Sun-god of the gods."
103. He was clothed with the aura of the Ten Gods, so exalted was his strength,
104. The Fifty Dreads were loaded upon him.
105. Anu formed and gave birth to the four winds,
106. He delivered them to him, "My son, let them whirl!"
107. He formed dust and set a hurricane to drive it,
108. He made a wave to bring consternation on Tia-mat.
109. Tia-mat was confounded; day and night she was frantic.
110. The gods took no rest, they . . . .
111. In their minds they plotted evil,
112. And addressed their mother Tia-mat,
113. "When Apsû, your spouse, was killed,
114. You did not go at his side, but sat quietly.
115. The four dreadful winds have been fashioned
116. To throw you into confusion, and we cannot sleep.
117. You gave no thought to Apsû, your spouse,
118. Nor to Mummu, who is a prisoner. Now you sit alone.
119. Henceforth you will be in frantic consternation!
120. And as for us, who cannot rest, you do not love us!
121. Consider our burden, our eyes are hollow.
122. Break the immovable yoke that we may sleep.
123. Make battle, avenge them!

124. [.....] .... reduce to nothingness!"

125. Tia-mat heard, the speech pleased her,

126. (She said,) "Let us make demons, [as you] have advised."

127. The gods assembled within her.

128. They conceived [evil] against the gods their begetters.

129. They ..... and took the side of Tia-mat,

130. Fiercely plotting, unresting by night and day,

131. Lusting for battle, raging, storming,

132. They set up a host to bring about conflict.

133. Mother Hubur, who forms everything,

134. Supplied irresistible weapons, and gave birth to giant serpents.

135. They had sharp teeth, they were merciless ....

136. With poison instead of blood she filled their bodies.

137. She clothed the fearful monsters with dread,

138. She loaded them with an aura and made them godlike.

139. (She said,) "Let their onlooker feebly perish,

140. May they constantly leap forward and never retire."

141. She created the Hydra, the Dragon, the Hairy Hero,

142. The Great Demon, the Savage Dog, and the Scorpion-man,

143. Fierce demons, the Fish-man, and the Bull-man,

144. Carriers of merciless weapons, fearless in the face of battle.

145. Her commands were tremendous, not to be resisted.

146. Altogether she made eleven of that kind.

147. Among the gods, her sons, whom she constituted her host,

148. She exalted Qingu, and magnified him among them.

149. The leadership of the army, the direction of the host,

150. The bearing of weapons, campaigning, the mobilization of conflict,

151. The chief executive power of battle, supreme command,

152. She entrusted to him and set him on a throne,

153. "I have cast the spell for you and exalted you in the host of the gods,

154. I have delivered to you the rule of all the gods.

155. You are indeed exalted, my spouse, you are renowned,

156. Let your commands prevail over all the Anunnaki."

157. She gave him the Tablet of Destinies and fastened it to his breast,

158. (Saying) "Your order may not be changed; let the utterance of your mouth be firm."

159. After Qingu was elevated and had acquired the power of Anuship,

160. He decreed the destinies for the gods, her sons:

161. "May the utterance of your mouths subdue the fire-god,

162. May your poison by its accumulation put down aggression."

Tablet II

1. Tia-mat gathered together her creation
2. And organized battle against the gods, her offspring.
3. Henceforth Tia-mat plotted evil because of Apsû
4. It became known to Ea that she had arranged the conflict.
5. Ea heard this matter,
6. He lapsed into silence in his chamber and sat motionless.
7. After he had reflected and his anger had subsided
8. He directed his steps to Anšar his father.
9. He entered the presence of the father of his begetter, Anšar,
10. And related to him all of Tia-mat's plotting.
11. "My father, Tia-mat our mother has conceived a hatred for us,
12. She has established a host in her savage fury.
13. All the gods have turned to her,
14. Even those you (pl.) begat also take her side
15. They . . . . . and took the side of Tia-mat,
16. Fiercely plotting, unresting by night and day,
17. Lusting for battle, raging, storming,
18. They set up a host to bring about conflict.
19. Mother H(ubur, who forms everything,
20. Supplied irresistible weapons, and gave birth to giant serpents.
21. They had sharp teeth, they were merciless.
22. With poison instead of blood she filled their bodies.
23. She clothed the fearful monsters with dread,
24. She loaded them with an aura and made them godlike.
25. (She said,) 'Let their onlooker feebly perish,
26. May they constantly leap forward and never retire.'
27. She created the Hydra, the Dragon, the Hairy Hero,
28. The Great Demon, the Savage Dog, and the Scorpion-man,
29. Fierce demons, the Fish-man, and the Bull-man,
30. Carriers of merciless weapons, fearless in the face of battle.
31. Her commands were tremendous, not to be resisted.
32. Altogether she made eleven of that kind.
33. Among the gods, her sons, whom she constituted her host,
34. She exalted Qingu and magnified him among them.
35. The leadership of the army, the direction of the host,
36. The bearing of weapons, campaigning, the mobilization of conflict,
37. The chief executive power of battle supreme command,
38. She entrusted to him and set him on a throne.

39. 'I have cast the spell for you and exalted you in the host of the gods,

40. I have delivered to you the rule of all the gods.

41. You are indeed exalted, my spouse, you are renowned,

42. Let your commands prevail over all the Anunnaki.'

43. She gave him the tablet of Destinies and fastened it to his breast,

44. (Saying) 'Your order may not be changed; let the utterance of your mouth be firm.'

45. After Qingu was elevated and had acquired the power of Anuship

46. He decreed the destinies for the gods, her sons:

47. 'May the utterance of your mouths subdue the fire-god,

48. May your poison by its accumulation put down aggression.'"

49. Anšar heard; the matter was profoundly disturbing.

50. He cried "Woe!" and bit his lip.

51. His heart was in fury, his mind could not be calmed.

52. Over Ea his son his cry was faltering.

53. "My son, you who provoked the war,

54. Take responsibility for whatever you alone have done!

55. You set out and killed Apsû,

56. And as for Tia-mat, whom you made furious, where is her equal?"

57. The gatherer of counsel, the learned prince,

58. The creator of wisdom, the god Nudimmud

59. With soothing words and calming utterance

60. Gently answered [his] father Anšar

61. "My father, deep mind, who decrees destiny,

62. Who has the power to bring into being and destroy,

63. Anšar, deep mind, who decrees destiny,

64. Who has the power to bring into being and to destroy,

65. I want to say something to you, calm down for me for a moment

66. And consider that I performed a helpful deed.

67. Before I killed Apsû

68. Who could have seen the present situation?

69. Before I quickly made an end of him

70. What were the circumstances were I to destroy him?"

71. Anšar heard, the words pleased him.

72. His heart relaxed to speak to Ea,

73. "My son, your deeds are fitting for a god,

74. You are capable of a fierce, unequalled blow . . [. . .]

75. Ea, your deeds are fitting for a god,

76. You are capable of a fierce, unequalled blow . . [. . .]

77. Go before Tia-mat and appease her attack,

78. . . [. . .] . . . her fury with [your] incantation."

79. He heard the speech of Anšar his father,

80. He took the road to her, proceeded on the route to her.

81. He went, he perceived the tricks of Tia-mat,

82. [He stopped], fell silent, and turned back.

83. [He] entered the presence of august Anšar

84. Penitently addressing him,

85. "[My father], Tia-mat's deeds are too much for me.

86. I perceived her planning, and [my] incantation was not equal (to it).

87. Her strength is mighty, she is full of dread,

88. She is altogether very strong, none can go against her.

89. Her very loud cry did not diminish,

90. [I became afraid] of her cry and turned back.

91. [My father], do not lose hope, send a second person against her.

92. Though a woman's strength is very great, it is not equal to a man's.

93. Disband her cohorts, break up her plans

94. Before she lays her hands on us."

95. Anšar cried out in intense fury,

96. Addressing Anu his son,

97. "Honored son, hero, warrior,

98. Whose strength is mighty, whose attack is irresistible

99. Hasten and stand before Tia-mat,

100. Appease her rage that her heart may relax

101. If she does not harken to your words,

102. Address to her words of petition that she may be appeased."

103. He heard the speech of Anšar his father,

104. He took the road to her, proceeded on the route to her.

105. Anu went, he perceived the tricks of Tia-mat,

106. He stopped, fell silent, and turned back.

107. He entered the presence of Anšar the father who begat him,

108. Penitently addressing him.

109. "My father, Tia-mat's [deeds] are too much for me.

110. I perceived her planning, but my [incantation] was not [equal] (to it).

111. Her strength is mighty, she is [full] of dread,

112. She is altogether very strong, no one [can go against her].

113. Her very loud noise does not diminish,

114. I became afraid of her cry and turned back.

115. My father, do not lose hope, send another person against her.

116. Though a woman's strength is very great, it is not equal to a man's.

117. Disband her cohorts, break up her plans,

118. Before she lays her hands on us."

119. Anšar lapsed into silence, staring at the ground,

120. He nodded to Ea, shaking his head.

121. The Igigi and all the Anunnaki had assembled,

122. They sat in tight-lipped silence.

123. No god would go to face .. [..]

124. Would go out against Tia-mat . . . . [..]

125. Yet the lord Anšar, the father of the great gods,

126. Was angry in his heart, and did not summon anyone.

127. A mighty son, the avenger of his father,

128. He who hastens to war, the warrior Marduk

129. Ea summoned (him) to his private chamber

130. To explain to him his plans.

131. "Marduk, give counsel, listen to your father.

132. You are my son, who gives me pleasure,

133. Go reverently before Anšar,

134. Speak, take your stand, appease him with your glance."

135. Be-l rejoiced at his father's words,

136. He drew near and stood in the presence of Anšar.

137. Anšar saw him, his heart filled with satisfaction,

138. He kissed his lips and removed his fear.

139. "My [father] do not hold your peace, but speak forth,

140. I will go and fulfil your desires!

141. [Anšar,] do not hold your peace, but speak forth,

142. I will go and fulfil your desires!

143. Which man has drawn up his battle array against you?

144. And will Tia-mat, who is a woman, attack you with (her) weapons?

145. [My father], begetter, rejoice and be glad,

146. Soon you will tread on the neck of Tia-mat!

147. [Anšar], begetter, rejoice and be glad,

148. Soon you will tread on the neck of Tia-mat!"

149. ["Go,] my son, conversant with all knowledge,

150. Appease Tia-mat with your pure spell.

151. Drive the storm chariot without delay,

152. And with a [..] which cannot be repelled turn her back."

153. Be-l rejoiced at his father's words,

154. With glad heart he addressed his father,

155. "Lord of the gods, Destiny of the great gods,

156. If I should become your avenger,

157. If I should bind Tia-mat and preserve you,

158. Convene an assembly and proclaim for me an exalted destiny.

159. Sit, all of you, in Upšukkinakku with gladness,

160. And let me, with my utterance, decree destinies instead of you.

161. Whatever I instigate must not be changed,

162. Nor may my command be nullified or altered."

Tablet III

1. Anšar opened his mouth

2. And addressed Kaka, his vizier,

3. "Vizier Kaka, who gratifies my pleasure,

4. I will send you to Lah(mu and Lah(amu.

5. You are skilled in making inquiry, learned in address.

6. Have the gods, my fathers, brought to my presence.

7. Let all the gods be brought,

8. Let them confer as they sit at table.

9. Let them eat grain, let them drink ale,

10. Let them decree the destiny for Marduk their avenger.

11. Go, be gone, Kaka, stand before them,

12. And repeat to them all that I tell you:

13. 'Anšar, your son, has sent me,

14. And I am to explain his plans.

15–52 = Tablet II, lines 11*–48 (* instead of "My father," put "Thus,")

53. I sent Anu, but he could not face her.

54. Nudimmud took fright and retired.

55. Marduk, the sage of the gods, your son, has come forward,

56. He has determined to meet Tia-mat.

57. He has spoken to me and said,

58–64 = Tablet II, lines 156–62* (* begin and end with single quotation marks: 'If ... altered.')

65. Quickly, now, decree your destiny for him without delay,

66. That he may go and face your powerful enemy."

67. Kaka went. He directed his steps

68. To Lah(mu and Lah(amu, the gods his fathers.

69. He prostrated himself, he kissed the ground before them,

70. He got up, saying to them he stood,

71–124 = III, 13–66

125. When Lah(h(a and Lah(amu heard, they cried aloud.

126. All the Igigi moaned in distress,

127. "What has gone wrong that she took this decision about us?

128. We did not know what Tia-mat was doing."

129. All the great gods who decree destinies

130. Gathered as they went,
131. They entered the presence of Anšar and became filled with [joy],
132. They kissed one another as they . [. .] in the assembly.
133. They conferred as they sat at table,
134. They ate grain, they drank ale.
135. They strained the sweet liquor through their straws,
136. As they drank beer and felt good,
137. They became quite carefree, their mood was merry,
138. And they decreed the fate for Marduk, their avenger.

Tablet IV

1. They set a lordly dais for him
2. And he took his seat before his fathers to receive kingship.
3. (They said,) "You are the most honored among the great gods,
4. Your destiny is unequaled, your command is like Anu's.
5. Marduk, you are the most honored among the great gods,
6. Your destiny is unequaled, your command is like Anu's.
7. Henceforth your order will not be annulled,
8. It is in your power to exalt and abase.
9. Your utterance is sure, your command cannot be rebelled against,
10. None of the gods will transgress the line you draw.
11. Shrines for all the gods need provisioning,
12. That you may be established where their sanctuaries are.
13. You are Marduk, our avenger,
14. We have given you kingship over the sum of the whole universe.
15. Take your seat in the assembly, let your word be exalted,
16. Let your weapons not miss the mark, but may they slay your enemies.
17. Be-l, spare him who trusts in you,
18. But destroy the god who set his mind on evil."
19. They set a constellation in the middle
20. And addressed Marduk, their son,
21. "Your destiny, Be-l, is superior to that of all the gods,
22. Command and bring about annihilation and re-creation.
23. Let the constellation disappear at your utterance,
24. With a second command let the constellation reappear."
25. He gave the command and the constellation disappeared,
26. With a second command the constellation came into being again.
27. When the gods, his fathers, saw (the effect of) his utterance,
28. They rejoiced and offered congratulation: "Marduk is the king!"
29. They added to him a mace, a throne, and a rod,

30. They gave him an irresistible weapon that overwhelms the foe:

31. (They said,) "Go, cut Tia-mat's throat,

32. And let the winds bear up her blood to give the news."

33. The gods, his fathers, decreed the destiny of Be-l,

34. And set him on the road, the way of prosperity and success.

35. He fashioned a bow and made it his weapon,

36. He set an arrow in place, put the bow string on.

37. He took up his club and held it in his right hand,

38. His bow and quiver he hung at his side.

39. He placed lightning before him,

40. And filled his body with tongues of flame.

41. He made a net to enmesh the entrails of Tia-mat,

42. And stationed the four winds that no part of her escape.

43. The South Wind, the North Wind, the East Wind, the West Wind,

44. He put beside his net, winds given by his father, Anu.

45. He fashioned the Evil Wind, the Dust Storm, Tempest,

46. The Four-fold Wind, the Seven-fold Wind, the Chaos-spreading Wind, the . . . . . Wind.

47. He sent out the seven winds that he had fashioned,

48. And they took their stand behind him to harass Tia-mat's entrails.

49. Be-l took up the Storm-flood, his great weapon,

50. He rode the fearful chariot of the irresistible storm.

51. Four steeds he yoked to it and harnessed them to it,

52. The Destroyer, The Merciless, The Trampler, The Fleet.

53. Their lips were parted, their teeth bore venom,

54. They were strangers to weariness, trained to sweep forward.

55. At his right hand he stationed raging battle and strife,

56. On the left, conflict that overwhelms a united battle array.

57. He was clad in a tunic, a fearful coat of mail,

58. And on has head he wore an aura of terror.

59. Be-l proceeded and set out on his way,

60. He set his face toward the raging Tia-mat.

61. In his lips he held a spell,

62. He grasped a plant to counter poison in his hand,

63. Thereupon they milled around him, the gods milled around him,

64. The gods, his fathers, milled around him, the gods milled around him.

65. Be-l drew near, surveying the maw of Tia-mat,

66. He observed the tricks of Qingu, her spouse.

67. As he looked, he lost his nerve,

68. His determination went and he faltered.

69. His divine aides, who were marching at his side,

70. Saw the warrior, the foremost, and their vision became dim.
71. Tia-mat cast her spell without turning her neck,
72. In her lips she held untruth and lies,
73. "[.] . . . .
74. In their [.] . they have assembled by you."
75. Be-l [lifted up] the Storm-flood, his great weapon,
76. And with these words threw it at the raging Tia-mat,
77. "Why are you aggressive and arrogant,
78. And strive to provoke battle?
79. The younger generation have shouted, outraging their elders,
80. But you, their mother, hold pity in contempt.
81. Qingu you have named to be your spouse,
82. And you have improperly appointed him to the rank of Anuship.
83. Against Anšar, king of the gods, you have stirred up trouble,
84. And against the gods, my fathers, your trouble is established.
85. Deploy your troops, gird on your weapons,
86. You and I will take our stand and do battle."
87. When Tia-mat heard this
88. She went insane and lost her reason.
89. Tia-mat cried aloud and fiercely,
90. All her lower members trembled beneath her.
91. She was reciting an incantation, kept reciting her spell,
92. While the (battle-)gods were sharpening their weapons of war.
93. Tia-mat and Marduk, the sage of the gods, came together,
94. Joining in strife, drawing near to battle.
95. Be-l spread out his net and enmeshed her;
96. He let loose the Evil Wind, the rear guard, in her face.
97. Tia-mat opened her mouth to swallow it,
98. She let the Evil Wind in so that she could not close her lips.
99. The fierce winds weighed down her belly,
100. Her inwards were distended and she opened her mouth wide.
101. He let fly an arrow and pierced her belly,
102. He tore open her entrails and slit her inwards,
103. He bound her and extinguished her life,
104. He threw down her corpse and stood on it.
105. After he had killed Tia-mat, the leader,
106. Her assembly dispersed, her host scattered.
107. Her divine aides, who went beside her,
108. In trembling and fear beat a retreat.
109. . . . . to save their lives,
110. But they were completely surrounded, unable to escape.

111. He bound them and broke their weapons,

112. And they lay enmeshed, sitting in a snare,

113. Hiding in corners, filled with grief,

114. Bearing his punishment, held in a prison.

115. The eleven creatures who were laden with fearfulness,

116. The throng of devils who went as grooms at her right hand,

117. He put ropes upon them and bound their arms,

118. Together with their warfare he trampled them beneath him.

119. Now Qingu, who had risen to power among them,

120. He bound and reckoned with the Dead Gods.

121. He took from him the Tablet of Destinies, which was not properly his,

122. Sealed it with a seal and fastened it to his own breast.

123. After the warrior Marduk had bound and slain his enemies,

124. Had . . . . the arrogant enemy . . . ,

125. Had established victory for Anšar over all his foes,

126. Had fulfilled the desire of Nudimmud,

127. He strengthened his hold on the Bound Gods,

128. And returned to Tia-mat, whom he had bound.

129. Be-l placed his feet on the lower parts of Tia-mat

130. And with his merciless club smashed her skull.

131. He severed her arteries

132. And let the North wind bear up (her blood) to give the news.

133. His fathers saw it and were glad and exulted;

134. They brought gifts and presents to him.

135. Be-l rested, surveying the corpse,

136. In order to divide the lump by a clever scheme.

137. He split her into two like a dried fish:

138. One half of her he set up and stretched out as the heavens.

139. He stretched the skin and appointed a watch

140. With the instruction not to let her waters escape.

141. He crossed over the heavens, surveyed the celestial parts,

142. And adjusted them to match the Apsû, Nudimmud's abode.

143. Be-l measured the shape of the Apsû

144. And set up Ešarra, a replica of Ešgalla.

145. In Ešgalla, Ešarra which he had built, and the heavens,

146. He settled in their shrines Anu, Enlil, and Ea.

Tablet V

1. He fashioned heavenly stations for the great gods,

2. And set up constellations, the patterns of the stars.

3. He appointed the year, marked off divisions,

4. And set up three stars each for the twelve months.

5. After he had organized the year,

6. He established the heavenly station of Ne-beru to fix the stars' intervals.

7. That none should transgress or be slothful

8. He fixed the heavenly stations of Enlil and Ea with it.

9. Gates he opened on both sides,

10. And put strong bolts at the left and the right.

11. He placed the heights (of heaven) in her (Tia-mat's) belly,

12. He created Nannar, entrusting to him the night.

13. He appointed him as the jewel of the night to fix the days,

14. And month by month without ceasing he elevated him with a crown,

15. (Saying,) "Shine over the land at the beginning of the month,

16. Resplendent with horns to fix six days.

17. On the seventh day the crown will be half size,

18. On the 15th day, halfway through each month, stand in opposition.

19. When Šamaš [sees] you on the horizon,

20. Diminish in the proper stages and shine backwards.

21. On the 29th day, draw near to the path of Šamaš,

22. . [. .] the 30th day, stand in conjunction and rival Šamaš.

23. I have (. . . .) . the sign, follow its track,

24. Draw near . . (. . . . .) give judgment.

25. . [. . . .] . Šamaš, constrain [murder] and violence,

26. . [. . . . .] . me.

* * * * * *

35. At the end [. . .

36. Let there [be] the 29th day [. . . "

37. After [he had . . . .] the decrees [. . .

38. The organization of front and . [. . .

39. He made the day [. . .

40. Let the year be equally [. . .

41. At the new year [. . .

42. The year . . . . . [. . .

43. Let there be regularly [. . .

44. The projecting bolt [. . .

45. After he had [. . .

46. The watches of night and day [. . .

47. The foam which Tia-mat [. . .

48. Marduk fashioned [. . .

49. He gathered it together and made it into clouds.

50. The raging of the winds, violent rainstorms,

51. The billowing of mist—the accumulation of her spittle—

52. He appointed for himself and took them in his hand.

53. He put her head in position and poured out .. [..] .

54. He opened the abyss and it was sated with water.

55. From her two eyes he let the Euphrates and Tigris flow,

56. He blocked her nostrils, but left ..

57. He heaped up the distant [mountains] on her breasts,

58. He bored wells to channel the springs.

59. He twisted her tail and wove it into the Durmah(u,

60. […] .. the Apsû beneath his feet.

61. [He set up] her crotch—it wedged up the heavens—

62. [(Thus) the half of her] he stretched out and made it firm as the earth.

63. [After] he had finished his work inside Tia-mat,

64. [He spread] his net and let it right out.

65. He surveyed the heavens and the earth .. [.] .

66. [..] their bonds . . . .

67. After he had formulated his regulations and composed [his] decrees,

68. He attached guide-ropes and put them in Ea's hands.

69. [The Tablet] of Destinies which Qingu had taken and carried,

70. He took charge of it as a trophy (?) and presented it to Anu.

71. [The .] . of battle, which he had tied on or had put on his head,

72. [.] . he brought before his fathers.

73. [Now] the eleven creatures to which Tia-mat had given birth and . . . ,

74. He broke their weapons and bound them (the creatures) to his feet.

75. He made images of them and stationed them at the [Gate] of the Apsû,

76. To be a sign never to be forgotten.

77. [The gods] saw it and were jubilantly happy,

78. (That is,) Lah(mu, Lah(amu and all his fathers.

79. Anšar [embraced] him and published abroad his title, "Victorious King,"

80. Anu, Enlil, and Ea gave him gifts.

81. Mother Damkina, who bore him, hailed him,

82. With a clean festal robe she made his face shine.

83. To Usmû, who held her present to give the news,

84. [He entrusted] the vizierate of the Apsû and the care of the holy places.

85. The Igigi assembled and all did obeisance to him,

86. Every one of the Anunnaki was kissing his feet.

87. They all [gathered] to show their submission,

88. […] . they stood, they bowed down, "Behold the king!"

89. His fathers […] . and took their fill of his beauty,

90. Be-l listened to their utterance, being girded with the dust of battle.

91. . [. . . . .] . . . .

92. Anointing his body with . […] cedar perfume.

93. He clothed himself in [his] lordly robe,

94. With a crown of terror as a royal aura.

95. He took up his club and held it in his right hand,

96. […] . he grasped in his left.

97. [. . . . .]

98. […] . he set his feet.

99. He put upon . […

100. The scepter of prosperity and success [he hung] at his side.

101. After [he had …] the aura [

102. He adorned(?) his sack, the Apsû, with a fearful [. .]

103. Was settled like . […

104. In [his] throne room […

105. In his cella […

106. Every one of the gods […

107. Lah(mu and Lah(amu . [. . . . . . .] .

108. Opened their mouths and [addressed] the Igigi gods,

109. "Previously Marduk was our beloved son,

110. Now he is your king, heed his command!"

111. Next, they all spoke up together,

112. "His name is Lugaldimmerankia, trust in him!"

113. When they had given kingship to Marduk,

114. They addressed to him a benediction for prosperity and success,

115. "Henceforth you are the caretaker of our shrine,

116. Whatever you command, we will do!"

117. Marduk opened his mouth to speak

118. And addressed the gods his fathers,

119. "Above the Apsû, the emerald abode,

120. Opposite Ešarra, which I built for you,

121. Beneath the celestial parts, whose floor I made firm,

122. I will build a house to be my luxurious abode.

123. Within it I will establish its shrine,

124. I will found my chamber and establish my kingship.

125. When you come up from the Apsû to make a decision

126. This will be your resting place before the assembly.

127. When you descend from heaven to make a decision

128. This will be your resting place before the assembly.

129. I shall call its name 'Babylon,' 'The Homes of the Great Gods,'

130. Within it we will hold a festival: that will be the evening festival.

131. [The gods], his fathers, [heard] this speech of his,

132. . [. . . . .] . they said,

133. "With regard to all that your hands have made,

134. Who has your [. . .]?

135. With regard to the earth that your hands have made,

136. Who has your [. . .]?

137. In Babylon, as you have named it,

138. Put our [resting place] for ever.

139. . [. . . . .] let them our bring regular offerings

140. . [. . . . .] . .

141. Whoever [. . .] our tasks which we . [. . .

142. Therein [. . . . .] its toil . [. . .

143. [. . . . .]

144. They rejoiced [. . . . .] . . [. . .

145. The gods . [. . . . .]

146. He who knows [. . . . .] . them

147. He opened [his mouth showing] them light,

148. . . [. . . . .] his speech . [.]

149. He made wide [. . . . .] . them [. . .

150. And . [. . . . .] . . . . .

151. The gods bowed down, speaking to him,

152. They addressed Lugaldimmerankia, their lord,

153. "Formerly, lord, [you were our beloved] son,

154. Now you are our king, . . [. . .]

155. He who . [.] . [.] preserved [us]

156. . . [. . .] the aura of club and scepter.

157. Let him conceive plans [. . . .] . . [. . .]

158. [.] . . [. . . . . . that] we . [. . ."

Tablet VI

1. When Marduk heard the gods' speech

2. He conceived a desire to accomplish clever things.

3. He opened his mouth addressing Ea,

4. He counsels that which he had pondered in his heart,

5. "I will bring together blood to form bone,

6. I will bring into being Lullû, whose name shall be 'man.'

7. I will create Lullû—man

8. On whom the toil of the gods will be laid that they may rest.

9. I will skillfully alter the organization of the gods:

10. Though they are honored as one, they shall be divided into two."

11. Ea answered, as he addressed a word to him,

12. Expressing his comments on the resting of the gods,

13. "Let one brother of theirs be given up.

14. Let him perish that people may be fashioned.

15. Let the great gods assemble

16. And let the guilty one be given up that they may be confirmed."

17. Marduk assembled the great gods,

18. Using gracious direction as he gave his order,

19. As he spoke the gods heeded him:

20. The king addressed a word to the Anunnaki,

21. "Your former oath was true indeed,

22. (Now also) tell me the solemn truth:

23. Who is the one who instigated warfare,

24. Who made Tia-mat rebel, and set battle in motion?

25. Let him who instigated warfare be given up

26. That I may lay his punishment on him; but you sit and rest."

27. The Igigi, the great gods, answered him,

28. That is, Lugaldimmerankia, the counsellor of the gods, the lord,

29. "Qingu is the one who instigated warfare,

30. Who made Tia-mat rebel and set battle in motion."

31. They bound him, holding him before Ea,

32. They inflicted the penalty on him and severed his blood-vessels.

33. From his blood he (Ea) created mankind,

34. On whom he imposed the service of the gods, and set the gods free.

35. After the wise Ea had created mankind

36. And had imposed the service of the gods upon them—

37. That task is beyond comprehension

38. For Nudimmud performed the creation with the skill of Marduk—

39. King Marduk divided the gods,

40. All the Anunnaki into upper and lower groups.

41. He assigned 300 in the heavens to guard the decrees of Anu

42. And appointed them as a guard.

43. Next he arranged the organization of the netherworld.

44. In heaven and netherworld he stationed 600 gods.

45. After he had arranged all the decrees,

46. And had distributed incomes among the Anunnaki of heaven and netherworld,

47. The Anunnaki opened their mouths

48. And addressed their lord Marduk,

49. "Now, lord, seeing you have established our freedom

50. What favor can we do for you?

51. Let us make a shrine of great renown:

52. Your chamber will be our resting place wherein we may repose.

53. Let us erect a shrine to house a pedestal

54. Wherein we may repose when we finish (the work)."

55. When Marduk heard this,

56. He beamed as brightly as the light of day,

57. "Build Babylon, the task you have sought.

58. Let bricks for it be molded, and raise the shrine!"

59. The Anunnaki wielded the pick.

60. For one year they made the needed bricks.

61. When the second year arrived,

62. They raised the peak of Esagil, a replica of the Apsû.

63. They built the lofty temple tower of the Apsû

64. And for Anu, Enlil, and Ea they established its . . as a dwelling.

65. He sat in splendor before them,

66. Surveying its horns, which were level with the base of Ešarra.

67. After they had completed the work on Esagil

68. All the Anunnaki constructed their own shrines.

69. 300 Igigi of heaven and 600 of the Apsû, all of them, had assembled.

70. Be-l seated the gods, his fathers, at the banquet

71. In the lofty shrine which they had built for his dwelling,

72. (Saying,) "This is Babylon, your fixed dwelling,

73. Take your pleasure here! Sit down in joy!

74. The great gods sat down,

75. Beer-mugs were set out and they sat at the banquet.

76. After they had enjoyed themselves inside

77. They held a service in awesome Esagil.

78. The regulations and all the rules were confirmed:

79. All the gods divided the stations of heaven and netherworld.

80. The college of the Fifty great gods took their seats,

81. The Seven gods of destinies were appointed to give decisions.

82. Be-l received his weapon, the bow, and laid it before them:

83. His divine fathers saw the net which he had made.

84. His fathers saw how skillfully wrought was the structure of the bow

85. As they praised what he had made.

86. Anu lifted it up in the divine assembly,

87. He kissed the bow, saying, "It is my daughter!"

88. Thus he called the names of the bow:

89.   "Long Stick" was the first; the second was, "May it hit the mark."

90.   With the third name, "Bow Star," he made it to shine in the sky,

91.   He fixed its heavenly position along with its divine brothers.

92.   After Anu had decreed the destiny of the bow,

93.   He set down a royal throne, a lofty one even for a god,

94.   Anu set it there in the assembly of the gods.

95.   The great gods assembled,

96.   They exalted the destiny of Marduk and did obeisance.

97.   They invoked a curse on themselves

98.   And took an oath with water and oil, and put their hands to their throats.

99.   They granted him the right to exercise kingship over the gods,

100. They confirmed him as lord of the gods of heaven and netherworld.

101. Anšar gave him his exalted name, Asalluh(i

102. "At the mention of his name, let us show submission!

103. When he speaks, let the gods heed him,

104. Let his command be superior in upper and lower regions.

105. May the son, our avenger, be exalted,

106. Let his lordship be superior and himself without rival.

107. Let him shepherd the black-heads, his creatures,

108. Let them tell of his character to future days without forgetting.

109. Let him establish lavish food offerings for his fathers,

110. Let him provide for their maintenance and be caretaker of their sanctuaries,

111. Let him burn incense to rejoice their sanctums.

112. Let him do on earth the same as he has done in heaven:

113. Let him appoint the black-heads to worship him.

114. The subject humans should take note and call on their gods,

115. Since he commands they should heed their goddesses,

116. Let food offerings be brought [for] (?) their gods and goddesses,

117. May they (?) not be forgotten, may they remember their gods,

118. May they . . . their . ., may they . . their shrines.

119. Though the black-heads worship some one, some another god,

120. He is the god of each and every one of us!

121. Come, let us call the fifty names

122. Of him whose character is resplendent, whose achievement is the same.

123. (1) MARDUK As he was named by his father Anu from his birth,

124. Who supplies pasturage and watering, making the stables flourish.

125. Who bound the boastful with his weapon, the storm flood,

126. And saved the gods, his fathers, from distress.

127. He is the son, the sun-god of the gods, he is dazzling,

128. Let them ever walk in his bright light.

129. On the peoples that he created, the living beings,

130. He imposed the service of the gods and they took rest.

131. Creation and annihilation, forgiveness and exacting the penalty

132. Occur at his command, so let them fix their eyes on him.

133. (2) Marukka: he is the god who created them

134. Who put the Anunnaki at ease, the Igigi at rest.

135. (3) Marutukku: he is the support of land, city, and its peoples,

136. Henceforth let the peoples ever heed him.

137. (4) Meršakušu: fierce yet deliberating, angry yet relenting,

138. His mind is wide, his heart is all-embracing.

139. (5) Lugaldimmerankia is the name by which we all called him,

140. Whose command we have exalted above that of the gods his fathers.

141. He is the lord of all the gods of heaven and netherworld,

142. The king at whose injunctions the gods in upper and lower regions shudder.

143. (6) Narilugaldimmerankia is the name we gave him, the mentor of every god,

144. Who established our dwellings in heaven and netherworld in time of trouble,

145. Who distributed the heavenly stations between Igigi and Anunnaki,

146. Let the gods tremble at his name and quake on their seats.

147. (7) Asalluh(i is the name by which his father Anu called him,

148. He is the light of the gods, a mighty hero,

149. Who, as his name says, is a protecting angel for god and land,

150. Who by a terrible combat saved our dwelling in time of trouble.

151. (8) Asalluh(i-Namtilla they called him secondly, the life-giving god,

152. Who, in accordance with the form (of) his (name), restored all the ruined gods,

153. The lord, who brought to life the dead gods by his pure incantation,

154. Let us praise him as the destroyer of the crooked enemies.

155. (9) Asalluh(i-Namru, as his name is called thirdly,

156. The pure god, who cleanses our character."

157. Anšar, Lah(mu, and Lah(amu (each) called him by three of his names,

158. Then they addressed the gods, their sons,

159. "We have each called him by three of his names,

160. Now you call his names, like us."

161. The gods rejoiced as they heard their speech,

162. In Upšuukkinaki they held a conference,

163. "Of the warrior son, our avenger,

164. Of the provisioner, let us extol the name."

165. They sat down in their assembly, summoning the destinies,

166. And with all due rites they called his name:

Tablet VII

1.   (10) Asarre, the giver of arable land who established plough-land,
2.   The creator of barley and flax, who made plant life grow.
3.   (11) Asaralim, who is revered in the counsel chamber, whose counsel excels,
4.   The gods heed it and grasp fear of him.
5.   (12) Asaralimnunna, the noble, the light of the father, his begetter,
6.   Who directs the decrees of Anu, Enlil, and Ea, that is Ninšiku.
7.   He is their provisioner, who assigns their incomes,
8.   Whose turban multiplies abundance for the land.
9.   (13) Tutu is he, who accomplishes their renovation,
10.   Let him purify their sanctuaries that they may repose.
11.   Let him fashion an incantation that the gods may rest,
12.   Though they rise up in fury, let them withdraw.
13.   He is indeed exalted in the assembly of the gods, his [fathers],
14.   No one among the gods can [equal] him.
15.   (14) Tutu-Ziukkinna, the life of [his] host,
16.   Who established the pure heavens for the gods,
17.   Who took charge of their courses, who appointed [their stations],
18.   May he not be forgotten among mortals, but [let them remember] his deeds.
19.   (15) Tutu-Ziku they called him thirdly, the establisher of purification,
20.   The god of the pleasant breeze, lord of success and obedience,
21.   Who produces bounty and wealth, who establishes abundance,
22.   Who turns everything scant that we have into profusion,
23.   Whose pleasant breeze we sniffed in time of terrible trouble,
24.   Let men command that his praises be constantly uttered, let them offer worship to him.
25.   As (16) Tutu-Agaku, fourthly, let humans extol him,
26.   Lord of the pure incantation, who brought the dead back to life,
27.   Who showed mercy on the Bound Gods,
28.   Who threw the imposed yoke on the gods, his enemies,
29.   And to spare them created mankind.
30.   The merciful, in whose power it is to restore to life,
31.   Let his words be sure and not forgotten
32.   From the mouths of the black-heads, his creatures.
33.   As (17) Tutu-Tuku, fifthly, let their mouth give expression to his pure spell,
34.   Who extirpated all the wicked by his pure incantation.
35.   (18) Šazu, who knew the heart of the gods, who saw the reins,
36.   Who did not let an evil-doer escape from him,
37.   Who established the assembly of the gods, who rejoiced their hearts,
38.   Who subjugated the disobedient, he is the gods' encompassing protection.

39. He made truth to prosper, he uprooted perverse speech,

40. He separated falsehood from truth.

41. As (19) Šazu-Zisi, secondly, let them continually praise him, the subduer of aggressors,

42. Who ousted consternation from the bodies of the gods, his fathers.

43. (20) Šazu-Suh(rim, thirdly, who extirpated every foe with his weapons,

44. Who confounded their plans and turned them into wind.

45. He snuffed out all the wicked who came against him,

46. Let the gods ever shout acclamations in the assembly.

47. (21) Šazu-Suh(gurim, fourthly, who established success for the gods, his fathers,

48. Who extirpated foes and destroyed their offspring,

49. Who scattered their achievements, leaving no part of them,

50. Let his name be spoken and proclaimed in the land.

51. As (22) Šazu-Zah(rim, fifthly, let future generations discuss him,

52. The destroyer of every rebel, of all the disobedient,

53. Who brought all the fugitive gods into the shrines,

54. Let this name of his be established.

55. As (23) Šazu-Zah(gurim, sixthly, let them altogether and everywhere worship him,

56. Who himself destroyed all the foes in battle.

57. (24) Enbilulu is he, the lord who supplies them abundantly,

58. Their great chosen one, who provides cereal offerings,

59. Who keeps pasturage and watering in good condition and established it for the land,

60. Who opened watercourses and distributed plentiful water.

61. (25) Enbilulu-Epadun, lord of common land and . . ., let them [call him] secondly,

62. Canal supervisor of heaven and netherworld, who sets the furrow,

63. Who establishes clean arable land in the open country,

64. Who directs irrigation ditch and canal, and marks out the furrow.

65. As (26) Enbilulu-Gugal, canal supervisor of the water courses of the gods, let them praise him thirdly,

66. Lord of abundance, profusion, and huge stores (of grain),

67. Who provides bounty, who enriches human habitations,

68. Who gives wheat, and brings grain into being.

69. (27) Enbilulu-H(egal, who accumulates abundance for the peoples . . . .

70. Who rains down riches on the broad earth, and supplies abundant vegetation.

71. (28) Sirsir, who heaped up a mountain on top of Tia-mat,

72. Who plundered the corpse of Tia-mat with [his] weapons,

73. The guardian of the land, their trustworthy shepherd,

74. Whose hair is a growing crop, whose turban is a furrow,

75. Who kept crossing the broad Sea in his fury,

76. And kept crossing over the place of her battle as though it were a bridge.

77. (29) Sirsir-Malah they named him secondly—so be it—

78. Tia-mat was his boat, he was her sailor.

79. (30) Gil, who ever heaps up piles of barley, massive mounds,

80. The creator of grain and flocks, who gives seed for the land.

81. (31) Gilima, who made the bond of the gods firm, who created stability,

82. A snare that overwhelmed them, who yet extended favors.

83. (32) Agilima, the lofty, who snatches off the crown, who takes charge of snow,

84. Who created the earth on the water and made firm the height of heaven.

85. (33) Zulum, who assigns meadows for the gods and divides up what he has created,

86. Who gives incomes and food-offerings, who administers shrines.

87. (34) Mummu, creator of heaven and underworld, who protects refugees,

88. The god who purifies heaven and underworld, secondly Zulummu,

89. In respect of whose strength none other among the gods can equal him.

90. (35) Gišnumunab, creator of all the peoples, who made the world regions,

91. Who destroyed Tia-mat's gods, and made peoples from part of them.

92. (36) Lugalabdubur, the king who scattered the works of Tia-mat, who uprooted her weapons,

93. Whose foundation is secure on the "Fore and Aft."

94. (37) Pagalguenna, foremost of all lords, whose strength is exalted,

95. Who is the greatest among the gods, his brothers, the most noble of them all.

96. (38) Lugaldurmah king of the bond of the gods, lord of Durmah(u,

97. Who is the greatest in the royal abode, infinitely more lofty than the other gods.

98. (39) Aranunna, counsellor of Ea, creator of the gods, his fathers,

99. Whom no god can equal in respect of his lordly walk.

100. (40) Dumuduku, who renews for himself his pure abode in Duku,

101. Dumuduku, without whom Lugalduku does not make a decision.

102. (41) Lugalšuanna, the king whose strength is exalted among the gods,

103. The lord, the strength of Anu, he who is supreme, chosen of Anšar.

104. (42) Irugga, who plundered them all in the Sea,

105. Who grasps all wisdom, is comprehensive in understanding.

106. (43) Irqingu, who plundered Qingu in . . . battle,

107. Who directs all decrees and establishes lordship.

108. (44) Kinma, the director of all the gods, who gives counsel,

109. At whose name the gods bend down in reverence as before a hurricane.

110. (45) Dingir-Esiskur—let him take his lofty seat in the House of Benediction,

111. Let the gods bring their presents before him

112. Until he receives their offerings.

113. No one but he accomplishes clever things

114. The four (regions) of black-heads are his creation,

115. Apart from him no god knows the measure of their days.

116. (46) Girru, who makes weapons hard (?),

117. Who accomplished clever things in the battle with Tia-mat,

118. Comprehensive in wisdom, skilled in understanding,

119. A deep mind, that all the gods combined do not understand.

120. Let (47) Addu be his name, let him cover the whole span of heaven,

121. Let him thunder with his pleasant voice upon the earth,

122. May the rumble fill (?) the clouds and give sustenance to the peoples below.

123. (48) Aša-ru, who, as his name says, mustered the Divine Fates

124. He indeed is the warden of absolutely all peoples.

125. As (49) Ne-beru let him hold the crossing place of heaven and underworld,

126. They should not cross above or below, but should wait for him.

127. Ne-beru is his star, which he caused to shine in the sky,

128. Let him take his stand on the heavenly staircase that they may look at him.

129. Yes, he who constantly crosses the Sea without resting,

130. Let his name be Ne-beru, who grasps her middle,

131. Let him fix the paths of the stars of heaven,

132. Let him shepherd all the gods like sheep,

133. Let him bind Tia-mat and put her life in mortal danger,

134. To generations yet unborn, to distant future days,

135. May he continue unchecked, may he persist into eternity.

136. Since he created the heavens and fashioned the earth,

137. Enlil, the father, called him by his own name, (50) 'Lord of the Lands.'"

138. Ea heard the names which all the Igigi called

139. And his spirit became radiant.

140. "Why! He whose name was extolled by his fathers

141. Let him, like me, be called (51) 'Ea.'

142. Let him control the sum of all my rites,

143. Let him administer all my decrees."

144. With the word "Fifty" the great gods

145. Called his fifty names and assigned him an outstanding position.

146. They should be remembered; a leading figure should expound them,

147. The wise and learned should confer about them,

148. A father should repeat them and teach them to his son,

149. One should explain them to shepherd and herdsman.

150. If one is not negligent to Marduk, the Enlil of the gods,

151. May one's land flourish, and oneself prosper,

152. (For) his word is reliable, his command unchanged,

153. No god can alter the utterance of his mouth.

154. When he looks in fury, he does not relent,

155. When his anger is ablaze, no god can face him.

156. His mind is deep, his spirit is all-embracing,

157. Before whom sin and transgression are sought out.

158. Instruction which a leading figure repeated before him (Marduk):

159.   He wrote it down and stored it so that generations to come might hear it.

160.   [..] . Marduk, who created the Igigi gods,

161.   Though they diminish . . . let them call on his name.

162.   . . . the song of Marduk,

163.   Who defeated Tia-mat and took kingship.

STUDY QUESTIONS REGARDING THE THREE CREATION STORIES

1.   How do the three versions of creation compare with each other?
2.   How are they different? In what ways are they similar?
3.   What kinds of information and ideas about the culture and gods do you think the authors may have been attempting to convey?
4.   What is monotheism?
5.   What is polytheism?
6.   What is henotheism?

Genesis Flood

Following the Genesis creation myths and other events (e.g., Cain and Abel, the development of Adam and Eve's lineage, the Tower of Babel, the story of the Nephilim, etc.), humankind and the rest of the created world spiraled downward through murder and other sinister acts. Many of these events culminate and contribute to a decision by the deity to destroy the world. The biblical writers explain that humankind is so out of control, Yahweh even repents for his creation.

> *The LORD saw that the wickedness of humankind was great in the earth, and that every inclination of the thoughts of their hearts was only continually evil. And the LORD was sorry that he made humankind on the earth, and it grieved him to his heart. So the LORD said, "I will blot out from the earth human beings I have created—people together with animals and creeping things and birds of the air, for I am sorry that I have made them." (Gen. 6:5–7).*

As a result, the deity decides to extinguish life on the earth with a great deluge. It will even wipe out humankind. Yet, there is one man that finds favor with him—Noah. The writers' first mention of Noah (6:8) is positive. He is a favorite of Yahweh.

> *But Noah found favor in the sight of the LORD (Gen. 6:8).*

This introduction explains that Yahweh likes him, and Noah is bound to do something good. The favorable descriptions continue:

> *Noah was a righteous man, blameless in his generation: Noah walked with God (Gen. 6:9).*

This is the ultimate high-praise presentation of the Noah figure—righteous, blameless, and he walked with God. Even Enoch, who the writers say lived 365 years, was taken up from the earth by the deity, and supposedly did not see death (5:18–21) did not receive accolades like this.

Many know or have heard the story of Noah and the flood. This narrative has inspired a number of movies (*The Bible: In the Beginning*, 1966; *Genesis: The Creation and the Flood* 1994; *Noah's Ark* [TV movie with Tony Danza], 1998; *Evan Almighty*, 2007; *Noah*, 2014) and has also generated inspirational songs ("Didn't it Rain"; "Rise and Shine"):

> The Lord told Noah there's gonna be a floody, floody
> The Lord told Noah to build him an arky, arky
> The animals, they came, they came in by twosies twosies
> It rained and poured for forty daysies, daysies
> ("Rise and Shine" lyrics)

> Didn't it rain children
> Talk about rain, oh my Lord
> Oh it rained forty days, and it rained forty nights
> ("Didn't It Rain" Lyrics)

The films and tunes are enjoyable and entertaining, but do they reflect what the writers state in the Genesis story? For instance, how long does the flood event last? Is the number two the only number associated with how the animals are boarded on the ark? Moreover, a close reading of the text reveals that much like in Genesis, at least two stories have been combined to generate this narrative. There are strong characteristics of the P and J sources, and possibly another, present.

Genesis 6:5–22

⁵ The LORD saw that the wickedness of humankind was great in the earth, and that every inclination of the thoughts of their hearts was only evil continually. And the LORD was sorry that he had made humankind on the earth, and it grieved him to his heart. So the LORD said, "I will blot out from the earth the human beings I have created—people together with animals and creeping things and birds of the air, for I am sorry that I have made them." But Noah found

favor in the sight of the LORD. These are the descendants of Noah. Noah was a righteous man, blameless in his generation; Noah walked with God. And Noah had three sons, Shem, Ham, and Japheth.

Now the earth was corrupt in God's sight, and the earth was filled with violence. And God saw that the earth was corrupt; for all flesh had corrupted its ways upon the earth. And God said to Noah, "I have determined to make an end of all flesh, for the earth is filled with violence because of them; now I am going to destroy them along with the earth. Make yourself an ark of cypress wood; make rooms in the ark, and cover it inside and out with pitch. This is how you are to make it: the length of the ark three hundred cubits, its width fifty cubits, and its height thirty cubits. Make a roof for the ark, and finish it to a cubit above; and put the door of the ark in its side; make it with lower, second, and third decks. For my part, I am going to bring a flood of waters on the earth, to destroy from under heaven all flesh in which is the breath of life; everything that is on the earth shall die. But I will establish my covenant with you; and you shall come into the ark, you, your sons, your wife, and your sons' wives with you. And of every living thing, of all flesh, you shall bring two of every kind into the ark, to keep them alive with you; they shall be male and female. Of the birds according to their kinds, and of the animals according to their kinds, of every creeping thing of the ground according to its kind, two of every kind shall come in to you, to keep them alive. Also take with you every kind of food that is eaten, and store it up; and it shall serve as food for you and for them." Noah did this; he did all that God commanded him.

Genesis 7:1–24

Then the LORD said to Noah, "Go into the ark, you and all your household, for I have seen that you alone are righteous before me in this generation. Take with you seven pairs of all clean animals, the male and its mate; and a pair of the animals that are not clean, the male and its mate; and seven pairs of the birds of the air also, male and female, to keep their kind alive on the face of all the earth. For in seven days I will send rain on the earth for forty days and forty nights; and every living thing that I have made I will blot out from the face of the ground." And Noah did all that the LORD had commanded him.

Noah was six hundred years old when the flood of waters came on the earth. And Noah with his sons and his wife and his sons' wives went into the ark to escape the waters of the flood. Of clean animals, and of animals that are not clean, and of birds, and of everything that creeps on the ground, two and two, male and female, went into the ark with Noah, as God had commanded Noah. And after seven days the waters of the flood came on the earth.

In the six hundredth year of Noah's life, in the second month, on the seventeenth day of the month, on that day all the fountains of the great deep burst forth, and the windows of the heavens were opened. The rain fell on the earth for forty days and forty nights. On the very same day Noah with his sons, Shem and Ham and Japheth, and Noah's wife and the three wives of his sons entered the ark, they and every wild animal of every kind, and all domestic animals of every kind, and every creeping thing that creeps on the earth, and every bird of every kind—every bird, every winged creature. They went into the ark with Noah, two and two of all flesh in which there was the breath of life. And those that entered, male and female of all flesh, went in as God had commanded him; and the LORD shut him in.

The flood continued forty days on the earth; and the waters increased, and bore up the ark, and it rose high above the earth. The waters swelled and increased greatly on the earth; and the ark floated on the face of the waters. The waters swelled so mightily on the earth that all the high mountains under the whole heaven were covered; the waters swelled above the mountains, covering them fifteen cubits deep. And all flesh died that moved on the earth, birds, domestic animals, wild animals, all swarming creatures that swarm on the earth, and all human beings; everything on dry land in whose nostrils was the breath of life died. He blotted out every living thing that was on the face of the ground, human beings and animals and creeping things and birds of the air; they were blotted out from the earth. Only Noah was left, and those that were with him in the ark. And the waters swelled on the earth for one hundred fifty days.

Genesis 8:1–22

¹ But God remembered Noah and all the wild animals and all the domestic animals that were with him in the ark. And God made a wind blow over the earth, and the waters subsided; the fountains of the deep and the windows of the heavens were closed, the rain from the heavens was restrained, and the waters gradually receded from the earth. At the end of one hundred fifty days the waters had abated; and in the seventh month, on the seventeenth day of the month, the ark came to rest on the mountains of Ararat. The waters continued to abate until the tenth month; in the tenth month, on the first day of the month, the tops of the mountains appeared.

⁶ At the end of forty days Noah opened the window of the ark that he had made and sent out the raven; and it went to and fro until the waters were dried up from the earth. Then he sent out the dove from him, to see if the waters had subsided from the face of the ground; but the dove found no place to set its foot, and it returned to him to the ark, for the waters were still on the face of the whole earth. So he put out his hand and took it and brought it into the ark with him. He waited another seven days, and again he sent out the dove from the ark; and the dove came back to him in the evening, and there in its beak was a freshly plucked olive leaf; so Noah knew that the waters had subsided from the earth. Then he waited another seven days, and sent out the dove; and it did not return to him any more.

¹³ In the six hundred first year, in the first month, on the first day of the month, the waters were dried up from the earth; and Noah removed the covering of the ark, and looked, and saw that the face of the ground was drying. In the second month, on the twenty-seventh day of the month, the earth was dry. Then God said to Noah, "Go out of the ark, you and your wife, and your sons and your sons' wives with you. Bring out with you every living thing that is with you of all flesh—birds and animals and every creeping thing that creeps on the earth—so that they may abound on the earth, and be fruitful and multiply on the earth." So Noah went out with his sons and his wife and his sons' wives. And every animal, every creeping thing, and every bird, everything that moves on the earth, went out of the ark by families.

²⁰ Then Noah built an altar to the LORD, and took of every clean animal and of every clean bird, and offered burnt offerings on the altar. And when the LORD smelt the pleasing odor, the LORD said in his heart, "I will never again curse the ground because of humankind, for the inclination of the human heart is evil from youth; nor will I ever again destroy every living creature as I have done. As long as the earth endures, seedtime and harvest, cold and heat, summer and winter, day and night, shall not cease."

Mesopotamian Flood Story

The Mesopotamian Story of the Flood appears in the *Epic of Gilgamesh*. There are various versions and translations (e.g., *The Epic of Gilgamesh*, Maureen G. Kovacs; *Gilgamesh: A New*

FIG. 4.3 The newly discovered Tablet V of the *Epic of Gilgamesh*. Meeting Humbaba, with Enkidu, at the Cedar Forest. The Sulaymaniyah Museum, Iraqi Kurdistan.

English Version, Stephen Mitchell; *Gilgamesh: The New Translation*, Gerald Davis.) There are also a number of oral Sumerian legends about Gilgamesh, the historical king of Uruk (2700–2500 BCE): "Gilgamesh and the Land of the Living," "Gilgamesh, Enkidu, and the Netherworld," and "The Death of Gilgamesh."

Keep in mind that writing did not appear in the ancient Near East until around 3500 BCE, with the advent of cuneiform. Thus, people orally shared entertaining stories, current events, important news, and information from and about surrounding cultures and peoples. It is easy to think that peoples in antiquity that did not read or write were uneducated and not intelligent. This is an unfair and uninformed assessment of cultures we hardly understand and peoples we don't know and will never meet. Evaluations like this are biased and ignorantly based on present flawed standards used to determine intelligence and aptitude. These measuring sticks do not work well when used on peoples we know little about. In many ways, it places those that use this approach in an assumed place of supremacy. They are attempting to explain intricacies about people that can no longer speak for themselves.

Consider the following about the peoples of antiquity. More than likely, members of most groups in the ancient Near East spoke several languages and dialects; those who were at least bilingual would have helped push information across borders and into cultures different from theirs. Mesopotamian oral legends were probably written down around 2300. There are also Old Babylonian texts (1900–1600 BCE). Old Babylonian authors combined select independent stories about Gilgamesh, a unified work; added a hymnic introduction; and chose as a central theme Gilgamesh's concerns with death and his desire to overcome it. J. Tigay, author of *The Evolution of the The Epic of Gilgamesh*, discusses how the death of Enkidu, Gilgamesh's treasured friend, motivates his quest to visit Utnapishtim to discuss eternal life (46–47).[1]

The *Epic of Gilgamesh* had gained international popularity by the Middle Babylonian Period (1600–1000 BCE). The prologue, the flood story, and tablet XII became a part of it at this time. The prologue introduces the instructional aspect of the *Epic*. The flood story comes directly from *Atrahasis*, the Akkadian/Babylonian flood epic. To summarize, the gods send a deluge to destroy humans, and the god Ea warns the only good human, Atrahasis, to build an ark and load two of every kind of animal to preserve human and animal life.

---

1   Tigay, J. *The Evolution of the The Epic of Gilgamesh*. Bolchazy-Carcucci: Wauconda. 2002, 46–7.

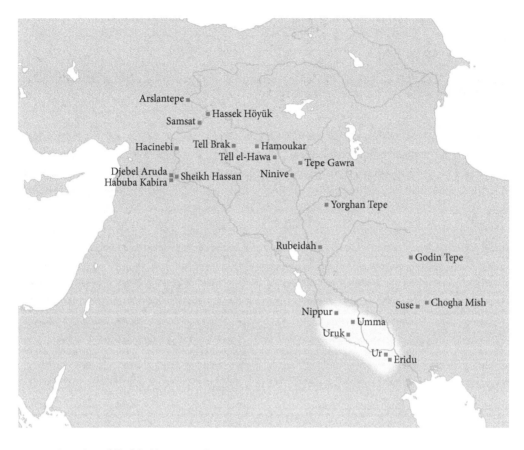

FIG. 4.4 Location of Uruk in Mesopotamia

In the *Epic of Gilgamesh*, the main character, Gilgamesh, meets a figure, Utnapishtim. Utnapishtim explains to Gilgamesh how he received eternal life from the gods. Utnapishtim functions in the same manner as the Atrahasis and Noah figures. He receives instructions to build a boat and take all the animals on the earth on board because a flood is coming. Once the rain stops, Utnapishtim, like Noah and Atrahasis, sends out birds to determine if he can vacate the boat. The gods are pleased with his obedience.

The Old Babylonian author/editor of the *Epic of Gilgamesh* created a new document out of existing oral and written traditions. The Middle Babylonian editors, who added to and transformed the Old Babylonian version, created their own document. They were not simply transmitters but literary creators. The history of this ancient text shows how each new edition of a text is a new literary piece, related genetically to its predecessor but also a literary piece worthy to stand on its own.

The Story of the Flood

You know the city Shurrupak, it stands on the banks of Euphrates? That city grew old and the gods that were in it were old. There was Anu, lord of the firmament, their father, and warrior Enlil their counsellor, Ninurta the helper, and Ennugi watcher over canals; and with them also was Ea. In those days the world teemed, the people multiplied, the world bellowed like a wild bull, and the great god was aroused by the clamour. Enlil heard the clamour and he said to the gods in council, "The uproar of mankind is intolerable and sleep is no longer possible by reason of the babel." So the gods agreed to exterminate mankind. Enlil did this, but Ea because of his oath warned me in a dream. He whispered their words to my house of reeds, "Reed-house, reed-house! Wall, O wall, hearken reed-house, wall reflect; O man of Shurrupak, son of Ubara-Tutu; tear down your house and build a boat, abandon possessions and look for life, despise worldly goods and save your soul alive. Tear down your house, I say, and build a boat. These are the measurements of the barque as you shall build her: let hex beam equal her length, let her deck be roofed like the vault that covers the abyss; then take up into the boat the seed of all living creatures."

When I had understood I said to my lord, "Behold, what you have commanded I will honour and perform, but how shall I answer the people, the city, the elders?" Then Ea opened his mouth and said to me, his servant, "Tell them this: I have learnt that Enlil is wrathful against me, I dare no longer walk in his land nor live in his city; I will go down to the Gulf to dwell with Ea my lord. But on you he will rain down abundance, rare fish and shy wild-fowl, a rich harvest-tide. In the evening the rider of the storm will bring you wheat in torrents."

In the first light of dawn all my household gathered round me, the children brought pitch and the men whatever was necessary. On the fifth day I laid the keel and the ribs, then I made fast the planking. The ground-space was one acre, each side of the deck measured one hundred and twenty cubits, making a square. I built six decks below, seven in all, I divided them into nine sections with bulkheads between. I drove in wedges where needed, I saw to the punt poles, and laid in supplies. The carriers brought oil in baskets, I poured pitch into the furnace and asphalt and oil; more oil was consumed in caulking, and more again the master of the boat took into his stores. I slaughtered bullocks for the people and every day I killed sheep. I gave the shipwrights wine to drink as though it were river water, raw wine and red wine and oil and white wine. There was feasting then as there is at the time of the New Year's festival; I myself anointed my head. On the seventh day the boat was complete.

Then was the launching full of difficulty; there was shifting of ballast above and below till two thirds was submerged. I loaded into her all that I had of gold and of living things, my family, my kin, the beast of the field both wild and tame, and all the craftsmen. I sent them on board, for the time that Shamash had ordained was already fulfilled when he said, "In the evening, when the rider of the storm sends down the destroying rain, enter the boat and batten her down." The time was fulfilled, the evening came, the rider of the storm sent down the rain. I looked out at the weather and it was terrible, so I too boarded the boat and battened her down. All was now complete, the battening and the caulking; so I handed the tiller to Puzur-Amurri the steersman, with the navigation and the care of the whole boat.

With the first light of dawn a black cloud came from the horizon; it thundered within where Adad, lord of the storm was riding. In front over hill and plain Shullat and Hanish, heralds of the storm, led on. Then the gods of the abyss rose up; Nergal pulled out the dams of the nether waters, Ninurta the war-lord threw down the dykes, and the seven judges of hell, the Annunaki, raised their torches, lighting the land with their livid flame. A stupor of despair went up to heaven when the god of the storm turned daylight to darkness, when he smashed the land like a cup. One whole

Selections from *Epic of Gilgamesh*, trans. Stephen Langdon, 1917.

day the tempest raged, gathering fury as it went, it poured over the people like the tides of battle; an imam could not see his brother nor the people be seen from heaven. Even the gods were terrified at the flood, they fled to the highest heaven, the firmament of Ann; they crouched against the walls, cowering like curs. Then Ishtar the sweet-voiced Queen of Heaven cried out like a woman in travail: "Alas the days -of old are turned to dust because I commanded evil; why did I command thus evil in the council of all the gods? I commanded wars to destroy the people, but are they not my people, for I brought them forth? Now like the spawn of fish they float in the ocean." The great gods of heaven and of hell wept, they covered their mouths.

For six days and six nights the winds blew, torrent and tempest and flood overwhelmed the world, tempest and flood raged together like warring hosts. When the seventh day dawned the storm from the south subsided, the sea grew calm, the, flood was stilled; I looked at the face of the world and there was silence, all mankind was turned to clay. The surface of the sea stretched as flat as a roof-top; I opened a hatch and the light fell on my face. Then I bowed low, I sat down and I wept, the tears streamed down my face, for on every side was the waste of water. I looked for land in vain, but fourteen leagues distant there appeared a mountain, and there the boat grounded; on the mountain of Nisir the boat held fast, she held fast and did not budge. One day she held, and a second day on the mountain of Nisir she held fast and did not budge. A third day, and a fourth day she held fast on the mountain and did not budge; a fifth day and a sixth day she held fast on the mountain. When the seventh day dawned I loosed a dove and let her go. She flew away, but finding no resting-place she returned. Then I loosed a swallow, and she flew away but finding no resting-place she returned. I loosed a raven, she saw that the waters had retreated, she ate, she flew around, she cawed, and she did not come back. Then I threw everything open to the four winds, I made a sacrifice and poured out a libation on the mountain top. Seven and again seven cauldrons I set up on their stands, I heaped up wood and cane and cedar and myrtle. When the gods smelled the sweet savour, they gathered like flies over the sacrifice. Then, at last, Ishtar also came, she lifted her necklace with the jewels of heaven that once Anu had made to please her. "O you gods here present, by the lapis lazuli round my neck I shall remember these days as I remember the jewels of my throat; these last days I shall not forget. Let all the gods gather round the sacrifice, except Enlil. He shall not approach this offering, for without reflection he brought the flood; he consigned my people to destruction."

When Enlil had come, when he saw the boat, he was wrath and swelled with anger at the gods, the host of heaven, "Has any of these mortals escaped? Not one was to have survived the destruction." Then the god of the wells and canals Ninurta opened his mouth and said to the warrior Enlil, "Who is there of the gods that can devise without Ea? It is Ea alone who knows all things." Then Ea opened his mouth and spoke to warrior Enlil, "Wisest of gods, hero Enlil, how could you so senselessly bring down the flood?"

STUDY QUESTIONS

1. How do the Genesis Flood stories and *Epic of Gilgamesh* compare with each other? How are they similar? How are they different?
2. What kind of information and ideas about the culture and gods do you think authors and editors may have been attempting to convey?

Credits

Fig. 4.1: Source: https://commons.wikimedia.org/wiki/File:The_ancient_Hebrew_conception_of_the_Universe.JPG.

Fig. 4.2: Source: https://commons.wikimedia.org/wiki/File:Early_Hebrew_Conception_of_the_Universe.png.

Fig. 4.3: Copyright © Osama Shukir Muhammed Amin (CC BY-SA 4.0) at https://commons.wikimedia.org/wiki/File:The_Newly_Discovered_Tablet_V_of_the_Epic_of_Gilgamesh._Meeting_Humbaba,_with_Enkidu,_at_the_Cedar_Forest._The_Sulaymaniyah_Museum,_Iraqi_Kurdistan.jpg.

Fig. 4.4: Copyright © Zunkir (CC BY-SA 3.0) at https://commons.wikimedia.org/wiki/File:Uruk_expansion.svg.

CHAPTER 5

Premonarchic Period

The Exodus and Settlement Period

TABLE 5.1 Outline of the Book of Exodus

Birth of Moses	Exod. 1:1–2:10
Moses in Midian	Exod. 2:11–4:17
Genealogy	Exod. 6:13–27
Plagues and the Origin of Passover	Exod. 6:28–12:30
Exodus from Egypt	Exod. 12:31–13:16
Crossing the Red Sea/Sea of Reeds	Exod. 13:17–15:21
Mount Sinai	Exod. 15:22–18:27
Ten Commandments	Exod. 19:1–20:21
Laws from Yahweh	Exod. 20:22–24:18
The Tabernacle	Exod. 25:31
Golden Calf Incident	Exod. 32:1–33:6
Tent Meeting	Exod. 33:7–23
The New Tablets	Exod. 34
Completion of the Tabernacle	Exod. 35:40

What comes to mind when you hear the word *exodus?* Exit? Departure? Leave? Get out? All of these are applicable to the story found in the Bible. The famous account describes the Hebrews living in horrific conditions under an oppressive, fearful pharaoh who doesn't like them. With the guidance of their god Yahweh and the leadership of Moses, Aaron, and Miriam, they are rescued in heroic fashion from the oppressive Egyptians and Pharaoh and head toward a land promised to their ancestors.

The Exodus story is known all over the world and is a part in various ways of a number of faith traditions. It is captivating, inspiring, and exciting. The underdog escapes, and lives are changed forever.

What does the word *exodus* mean? The origin is Latin, "going out," or from the Greek *exodus*, "a marching out, going out." Most definitions explain that it is a mass departure or emigration; a going out, usually of a large number of people. For this discussion, the term *Exodus* refers specifically to the event involving the Hebrews and Moses. Although it is an essential part of the development of the Hebrew Bible/Old Testament, the writers do not actually use the term to label the event.

We enter the story during a time in Egypt that is terrible for the Hebrews. This was in contrast to the period when Joseph was part of the leadership. The Exodus writers let us know early that things are not as they once were in this popular African land.

There arose a king in Egypt that did not know Joseph. (Exod. 1:8)

One can almost hear the dramatic music playing to indicate that something traumatic is on the horizon. Remember, at the end of Genesis, everything is lovely in Egypt. Joseph, a Hebrew, has made his way to becoming second in command in Egypt. After enduring a number of precarious, threatening situations, he climbed his way to the top. Sadly, Joseph had had to forsake his family, but finally they are reconciled in Egypt. The family became part of the rich and powerful. Joseph lived until the ripe age of 110 years old. Interestingly, although he was a Hebrew, the writers explain that he was buried according to the customs of the wealthy in Egypt during this time.

And Joseph died, being one hundred ten years old; he was embalmed and placed in a coffin in Egypt. (Gen. 50:26)

Before Joseph went the way of all flesh, it appears that life in Egypt was good for the Hebrews.

However, a new ruler comes to power in Egypt. This position is often referred to as the king or pharaoh. We have a solid understanding of the term *king*, a leadership position found in many cultures around the world, but what does *pharaoh* mean? *Pharaoh* was not a term used consistently in Egyptian culture. It becomes a part of the vocabulary and culture during the First Dynasty (ca. 3150 BCE) and lasts until the Macedonian Dynasty, roughly 305 BCE. The term itself comes from the Egyptian hieroglyph for "great house."

Although we have encountered the land of Egypt in earlier discussion and in the Genesis stories, a few words are in order regarding this magnificent land. It may be apparent to most, but at times it must be reiterated that Egypt is a part of the African continent. It is as much African as any other. Also, the country does have other names. It was also called *Kemet* ("Black Land"), *Aegyptos* (Greek), and *Mitzraim* (Hebrew).

As mentioned previously, there is also some debate regarding who was pharaoh at the time of the Exodus. The prevailing view is that it was Ramesses the II (1303–1213 BCE; reigned 1279–1213 BCE). The other possible contender is his father, Seti I (ca. 1294–1279 BCE). Most agree that it would have been Ramesses II.

FIG. 5.1 **Seti I**

FIG. 5.2 **Ramesses II**

According to the Exodus story, the writers express that Pharaoh was xenophobic toward the Hebrews (*xenophobia* is the fear and hatred of strangers or foreigners or anything that is unknown, foreign, or different). During his reign, he desires to wipe out the Hebrews and develops a cunning means to exterminate them. He institutes genocide. Pharaoh despises these people, but he's also afraid of them. Take note of how his methodical idea of annihilation develops.

> *Pharaoh said to his people, "Look, the Israelite [Hebrew] people*
> *are more numerous and more powerful than we." (Exod. 1:9).*

He's scared to death and also intimidated by the growing number of Hebrews. There are more people around Pharaoh that are different from him than of his own people, and he even interprets these others as being more powerful or at least having the potential to be. The writers don't elaborate with any useful detail about this power, but Pharaoh is definitely concerned about it. He goes on about what to do and why his fear is "justified."

> *"Come, let us deal shrewdly with them, or they will increase and,*
> *in the event of war, join our enemies and fight against us and*
> *escape from the land." (Exod. 1:10)*

Basically, the Pharaoh says, "Let's go put these folks in their place, because they will continue to grow in numbers. And we definitely can't have that. They might get smart and start partnering with people that we don't like. They could eventually become a force. They might even escape. We have to do something about this." So what does he decide to do?

> *Therefore, they set taskmasters over them to oppress them with forced labor. They built supply cities, Pithom and Rameses, for Pharaoh. (Exod. 1:11)*

To move his genocide forward, Pharaoh continues to denigrate the Hebrews and requires that all male children must be killed as soon as they are born. He gives this command to everyone, but he places tremendous pressure on the midwives to murder the male children as soon as they are born.

> *The king of Egypt said to the Hebrew midwives, one of whom was named Shiphrah and the other Puah, "When you act as midwives to the Hebrew women, and see them on the birthstool, if it is a boy, kill him; but if it is a girl, she shall live." (Exod. 1:15–16)*

> *Then Pharaoh commanded all his people, "Every boy that is born to the Hebrews you shall throw into the Nile, but you shall let every girl live." (Exod. 1:22)*

This is a very dangerous directive. Pharaoh is determined to annihilate an entire race of people for what he thought were legitimate reasons. Moreover, it's interesting that the biblical writers do not provide any voice from those in Pharaoh's administration or those serving under him standing to oppose this human injustice.

Yet this is the setting for Moses to enter the narrative. Moses does not come to his family by way of a barren motif, but the precarious scene is set as one in which he should not survive. In a barren motif, the mother supposedly cannot become pregnant; thus she cannot give birth. In this dire situation created by Pharaoh's xenophobia, it might be best that a mother not give birth, especially to a male child. And yet Moses's mother does. Just like the special figures Isaac, Joseph, and others came from women who were barren and overcame tremendous trials, the birth of Moses takes place in the midst of a tumultuous circumstance. He too is destined for a very unique life.

An artifact that would have been a part of African culture during this time is often overlooked—the birthstool. What is a birthstool?

> *The king of Egypt said to the Hebrew midwives, one of whom was named Shiphrah and the other Puah, "When you act as midwives to the Hebrew women, and see them on the birthstool, if it is a boy, kill him; but if it is a girl, she shall live." (Exod. 1:15–16)*

A birthstool or birthing chair is known in many cultures around the world. It is a device that allows a woman to squat while upright to assist in the birthing process. There are often arms on the chair that the woman can grip for leverage. The construction of the chair often gives the woman the option to brace her feet on the ground as well.

The writers explain that Moses was born to Levite parents in the midst of this genocide. Moses's parents—especially his mother—demonstrate unconditional love for their son. They know that he is destined to be murdered if he remains with them, so they have to circumvent this somehow. Note that they do not name him when he is born. He is referred to as *son, he,* and *child.* Is it possible that they do not give him a name out of fear of becoming too attached because he might be killed? Nevertheless, once the mother can hide him no longer, she places him in a carefully constructed basket and puts it in the Nile. They aren't sure where it will go, but his sister Miriam tracks it to see what will happen.

Pharaoh's daughter sees the basket and has one of her attendants bring it to her. His sister interjects herself into the situation to aid her infant brother. She offers to get a Hebrew woman to nurse the child, and the Pharaoh's daughter agrees that this is a good idea. Who does Miriam get to nurse the child? Their mother. The Pharaoh's daughter even pays the mother for nursing her own child. The child still does not have a name. The writers state that:

> When the child grew up, she [the mother] brought him to Pharaoh's daughter, and she took him as her son. She named him Moses, "because," she said, "I drew him out of the water." (Exod. 2:10)

Now we have a situation that is fascinating and often overlooked. Scholar Judy Fentress-Williams addresses this in her article, "Moses Has Two Mommies." She is on point. Moses has his birth mother, but the Pharaoh's daughter also claims him, or in actuality, adopts him as her son. Furthermore, she is the one who gave him his name. Fentress-Williams explains:

> Pharaoh's daughter rescues and names the child, making him her own. His name, Moses, works across language lines. His Egyptian mother named him Moses because "I drew him out of the water" (2:10). In Egyptian, the name Moses is likely derived from Thutmose, meaning "child of." In Hebrew, it means "the one who draws out," not "one drawn out" as Pharaoh's daughter claims.[1]

---

1   Fentress-Williams, J. "Moses Has Two Mommies" in *The Africana Bible: Reading Israel's Scriptures from Africa and the African Diaspora.* Hugh R. Page, Jr. ed., Minneapolis: Fortress. 2010, 82-3.

She also adds to her points and poses an interesting question:

> *Moses was nurtured by two women and most likely loved them both. As a result, he had two languages, two cultures, and two peoples. His upbringing demanded multiple consciousness. If he was connected to two peoples, how did he understand the prophetic words he uttered, "Let my people go"? (83)*

Understand that the birth and the situation into which Moses was born closely resembles another figure from the ancient Near East—the ruler Sargon of Akkad. The story of Sargon dates to ca. 2500 BCE. Following is an excerpt from his story:

> *Sargon, strong king, king of Agade, am I. My mother was a high priestess, my father I do not know. My paternal kin inhabit the mountain region. My city (of birth) is Azupiranu, which lies on the bank of the Euphrates. My mother, a high priestess, conceived me, in secret she bore me. She placed me in a reed basket, with bitumen she caulked my hatch. She abandoned me to the river from which I could not escape. The river carried me along: to Aqqi, the water drawer, it brought me. Aqqi, the water drawer,*

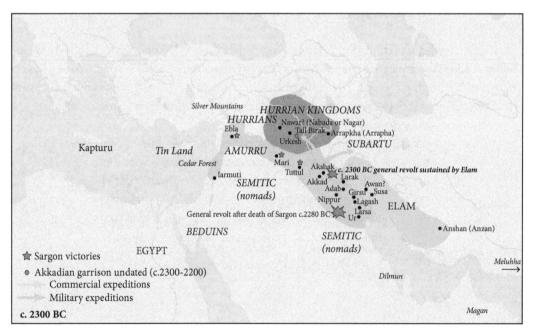

FIG. 5.3 **Map of Akkad in the 3rd Millennium**

when immersing his bucket lifted me up. Aqqi, the water drawer, raised me as adopted son. Aqqi, the water drawer, set me to his garden work. During my garden work, Istar loved me (so that) 55 years I ruled as king.[2]

The Call of Moses

In chapter 3 of Exodus, we find Moses working as a shepherd. Following his survival in the midst of chaos, he has now become a prince, murderer, fugitive, and husband (Exod. 2:11–2:25). Moses has married one of the seven daughters of Jethro, a priest in the land of Midian. Moses is now taking care of his father-in-law's flock (the writers do not indicate what kind of animals, but they are probably sheep or goats) on Mount Horeb or Mount Sinai, also known as the "mountain of God." As Moses leads the animals, he witnesses an interesting but not uncommon site—a burning bush. However, this bush is different because it is not being consumed. Also, an angel of Yahweh appears from the bush to Moses and calls him. He turns, sees this sight or *theophany*, responds, and receives a command and message:

"Do not come near; take your sandals off your feet, for the place on which your are standing is holy ground." And he said, "I am the God of your father, the God of Abraham, the God of Isaac, and the God of Jacob." (Exod. 3:5–6)

FIG. 5.4 **Image of Moses**

---

2   (Lewis, B. "The Sargon Legend." *American Schools of Oriental Research, 1978, 36–56.*

Yahweh and Moses then have a conversation about the plight of the people—Yahweh's people, the children of Israel—and the need to bring them out of Egypt. As one might expect, Moses is afraid; he doubts that he can do the job, and though he tries several times to wriggle his way out of the assignment through excuses about his inadequacy and lack of preparation, Yahweh will not let him escape. The writers have carefully walked us through the precariousness surrounding Moses's birth, his salvation due to the love and compassion of a number of women, and the apex of this moment in which he is charged to deliver the people from which he comes. His brother Aaron accompanies him. Moses has:

1. been divinely chosen for this specific task.
2. been empowered by the divine being Yahweh.
3. been given specific instructions regarding how to complete this task.
4. been given physical assistance with the accompaniment of his brother Aaron.

Once Moses goes back to Egypt and confronts Pharaoh, the struggle for power and freedom begins. Pharaoh, who is viewed as a deity, is in competition with the deity of the Israelites, Yahweh. Consequently, a pattern is established:

1. Moses and Aaron make a request: "Let my people go."
2. Pharaoh refuses.
3. Moses predicts a plague.
4. The plague happens, and Pharaoh cannot stop it.
5. Moses steps in, prays, and the plague ends. Pharaoh says the Israelites can go.
6. Pharaoh changes his mind ("Yahweh hardens his heart.")
7. Pattern starts again with Moses approaching Pharaoh requesting freedom for his people.

There are ten plagues:

1. Exod. 7:14–24 River turned to blood
2. Exod. 7:25–8:15 Frogs
3. Exod. 8:16–19 Lice or Gnats
4. Exod. 8:20–32 Flies
5. Exod. 9:1–7 Diseased livestock
6. Exod. 9:8–12 Boils
7. Exod. 9:13–35 Thunderstorm of hail
8. Exod. 10:1–20 Locusts
9. Exod. 10:21–29 Darkness for three days
10. Exod. 11:1–12:36 Death of firstborn

The final plague, the death of firstborn, is the zenith and makes the Pharaoh finally permit the Israelites to leave. It is also here that we see the impetus for Passover (Exod. 12).

The Exodus Travels

Moses led the Israelites out of Egypt, but there was no road map, no MapQuest, no GPS, to tell them where to go. They were no longer under Egyptian oppression. They were "free." But where were they going? They understood that Yahweh was with them. The deity was represented by a cloud during the day and a pillar of fire at night (Exod. 13:20–22). Thus, when they were uncertain about the deity's presence, they simply had to look up.

There of course is the famous part of the Exodus story of the Israelites and the crossing of water. The writers describe the large body of water miraculously opening or splitting so that the Israelites were able to cross on dry land. Once they had crossed and the Egyptian army entered, the walls of water came back together, destroying the Egyptian army. There have been some attempts to explain possibilities of how this event may have taken place. Many will classify it as inexplicable. At this point, there is no archaeological evidence connected with this event. However, one explanation is that there may have been strong winds blowing at the time, which exposed marsh areas or dry land, which would have provided a means to walk across.

There is also some question regarding whether the event took place at the Red Sea or some other location. The other location under consideration is *yam suph*, which translates as Sea of Reeds. One of the primary reasons is the composition of this body of water. It contains marsh areas, which would make it possible for people to cross, as well as impeding the travel of Egyptian chariots.

Yet, although the Israelites were out of the clutches of Pharaoh and the harsh treatments at the hands of Egyptians, there were issues and complaints throughout their travels through the Sinai wilderness. This is called a *murmuring motif*. In this motif, the Israelites often complain when in uncomfortable situations. Moses then speaks to Yahweh on their behalf. Consequently, Yahweh delivers them. However, punishment from the deity was sometimes involved. On several occasions, there were complaints about the lack of food, water, or shelter. There were arguments over which way to go. Their problems sounded much like a family trip, with children complaining that they were hungry and tired and constantly asking the question, "Are we there yet?"

> *When they came to Marah, they could not drink the water of Marah because it was bitter; therefore it was named Marah. And the people grumbled against Moses, saying, "What shall we drink?" (Exod. 15:23–24)*

> *The people quarreled with Moses, and said, "Give us water to drink." Moses said to them, "Why do you quarrel with me? Why do you test the LORD?" But the people thirsted there for water; and the people grumbled against Moses and said, "Why did you bring us out of Egypt, to kill us and our children and our livestock*

with thirst?" So Moses cried to the LORD, "What shall I do with this people? They are almost ready to stone me." (Exod. 17:2–4)

And the whole congregation of the people of Israel grumbled against Moses and Aaron in the wilderness., and the people of Israel said to them, 'Would that we had died by the hand of the LORD in the land of Egypt, when we sat by the meat pots and ate bread to the full, for you have brought us into this wilderness to kill this whole assembly with hunger." (Exod. 16:2–3)

In the evening quail came up and covered the camp, and in the morning dew lay around the camp. And when the dew had gone up, there was on the face of the wilderness a fine, flake-like thing, fine as frost on the ground. (Exod. 16:13–14)

Yahweh also protected them in battle during their travels. At one point during their journey, the Israelites cross an area occupied by the Amalekites, and there is a conflict. Moses asks Joshua to choose men to fight the Amalekites.

Moses said to Joshua, "Choose for us men, and go out and fight with Amalek. Tomorrow I will stand on the top of the hill with the staff of God in my hand." So Joshua did as Moses told him, and fought with Amalek, while Moses, Aaron, and Hur went up to the top of the hill. Whenever Moses held up his hand, Israel prevailed, and whenever he lowered his hand, Amalek prevailed. (Exod. 17:9–11)

Development of the Law and the Law Codes

The writers describe an intimate encounter Moses has with Yahweh and other events that took place on Mount Sinai. The most well known is Yahweh giving the Ten Commandments. While the Israelites are encamped at the bottom of Mount Sinai, Moses is communicating with Yahweh (Exod.19:2–ff.). The writers describe a cataclysmic event, with thunder, lightning, and a blast from a shofar (ram's horn) that scared the people. In the midst of this, the people dare not approach the mountain lest the deity chastise them.

On the morning of the third day there was thunder and lightning, as well as a thick cloud on the mountain, and a blast of a trumpet so loud that all the people who were in the camp trembled. Moses brought the people out of the camp to meet God. They took their stand at the foot of the mountain. Now Mount Sinai was wrapped in smoke, because the LORD had descended upon it in fire; the smoke went up like the smoke of a kiln, while the whole mountain shook violently. As the blast of the trumpet grew louder and louder, Moses would speak and God would answer him in thunder. When the LORD descended upon Mount Sinai, to the top of the mountain, the LORD summoned Moses to the top of the mountain, and Moses went up. Then the LORD said to Moses, "Go down and warn the people not to break through to the LORD to look; otherwise many of them will perish. Even the priests who approach the LORD must consecrate themselves or the LORD will break out against them." Moses said to the LORD, "The people are not permitted to come up to Mount Sinai; for you yourself warned us, saying, 'Set limits around the mountain and keep it holy.'" The LORD said to him, "Go down, and come up bringing Aaron with you; but do not let either the priests or the people break through to come up to the LORD; otherwise he will break out against them." So Moses went down to the people and told them. (Exod. 19:16–25)

In the midst of this, the deity of Israel shares with Moses how the Israelites should conduct themselves and interact with each other and outsiders. The communal and personal statutes given will help to shape Israelite culture. The people are to hear and understand Yahweh's place and relation to them ("Hear O Israel: the LORD is our God, the LORD alone" Deut. 6:4). This statement, of course, reflects later theological and cultural development and editing, but it says what transpires between the deity and Moses on Mount. Sinai. The bottom line is that if anyone is going to belong to this community, they are to be obedient, and hereby they will know and comprehend the laws regarding how to do it. Moses at this time receives the Decalogue, or Ten Commandments (Exod. 20:1–17).

Then God spoke all these words

[2] I am the LORD your God, who brought you out of the land of Egypt, out of the house of slavery; you shall have no other gods before me.

[4] You shall not make for yourself an idol, whether in the form of anything that is in heaven above, or that is on the earth beneath, or that is in the water under the earth. You shall not bow down to them or worship them; for I the LORD your God am a jealous God, punishing children for the iniquity of parents, to the third and the fourth generation of those who reject me, but showing steadfast love to the thousandth generation of those who love me and keep my commandments.

[7] You shall not make wrongful use of the name of the LORD your God, for the LORD will not acquit anyone who misuses his name.

[8] Remember the sabbath day, and keep it holy. Six days you shall labor and do all your work. But the seventh day is a sabbath to the LORD your God; you shall not do any work—you, your son or your daughter, your male or female slave, your livestock, or the alien resident in your towns. For in six days the LORD made heaven and earth, the sea, and all that is in them, but rested the seventh day; therefore the LORD blessed the sabbath day and consecrated it.

[12] Honor your father and your mother, so that your days may be long in the land that the LORD your God is giving you.

[13] You shall not murder.

[14] You shall not commit adultery.

[15] You shall not steal.

[16] You shall not bear false witness against your neighbor.

[17] You shall not covet your neighbor's house; you shall not covet your neighbor's wife, or male or female slave, or ox, or donkey, or anything that belongs to your neighbor.

Note that the laws are presented in an apodictic (established or beyond dispute) style. This is different from the casuistic or "if...then" types found in Exodus 21 and later:

> *When a man sells his daughter as a slave, she shall not go out as the male slaves do. If she does not please her master, who designated her for himself, then he shall let her be redeemed; he shall have no right to sell her to a foreign people, since he has dealt unfairly with her. (Exod.21:7–8)*

Understand that the Israelites and others in the ancient Near East did not live in a vacuum. Interaction between peoples prompted the sharing of cultural practices, exchange of ideas, styles of government, religious practices, interpretation of deities, and other things. A close look at the laws and ordinance of Israel appear to reflect the influence of the Code of Hammurabi and possibly other Mesopotamian codes of law. The idea of "an for an eye" (principle of lex talinois) is a fundamental element in both Hammurabi's Code and the laws of Israel.

Interestingly, Israelite law paid special attention to the poor and the handling of debt. This was an important factor in shaping the culture. While people had different tasks, occupations, and duties, the laws appear to exhibit some aspects of fairness when it comes to debt. The laws made sure that people were not enslaved because they owed money or fell on hard times.

Exod. 21:2 When you buy a male Hebrew slave, he shall serve six years, but in the seventh he shall go out a free person, without debt.

Deut. 15:1 Every seventh year you shall grant a remission of debts. And this is the manner of the remission: every creditor shall remit the claim that is held against a neighbor, not exacting it of a neighbor who is a member of the community, because the LORD's remission has been proclaimed.

Lev. 19:9-10 When you reap the harvest of your land, you shall not reap to the very edges of your field, or gather the gleanings of your harvest. 10 You shall not strip your vineyard bare, or gather the fallen grapes of your vineyard; you shall leave them for the poor and the alien: I am the LORD your God.

Lev. 25:35 If any of your kin fall into difficulty and become dependent on you, you shall support them; they shall live with you as though resident aliens. Do not take interest in advance or otherwise make a profit from them, but fear your God; let them live with you. You shall not lend them your money at interest taken in advance, or provide them food at a profit.

There are seven major bodies of law that determined how Israel was goverened:

1. Decalogue: Exod. 20:1–17; Deut. 5:6–21
2. Covenant Code: Exod. 20:18–23:33
3. Ritual Decalogue: Exod. 34:11–26
4. Deuteronomic Code: Deut. 12–26
5. Holiness Code: Lev. 17–26
6. Curses Code: Deut. 27:14–26

Covenant Renewal Ceremony

Summary of the Covenant Renewal Ceremony

At Mount Sinai, Moses leads the people in rededicating themselves to Yahweh. This is to remind them of their obligations and commitments. They are moving toward the promised land of Canaan, so they must be prepared. The people must understand that Yahweh is their leader, their judge. Moses reminds them of their journey and who is responsible for them getting to this point. To do this, Moses:

- brings the people of Israel together;
- reads the law out loud to the people;
- has the people hear the law and respond that they are rededicated to the law;
- and the people participate in a blood sacrifice.

> *Moses came and told the people all the words of the LORD and all the ordinances; and all the people answered with one voice, and said, "All the words that the LORD has spoken we will do." And Moses wrote down all the words of the LORD. He rose early in the morning, and built an altar at the foot of the mountain, and set up twelve pillars, corresponding to the twelve tribes of Israel. He sent young men of the people of Israel, who offered burnt offerings and sacrificed oxen as offerings of well-being to the LORD. Moses took half of the blood and put it in basins, and half of the blood he dashed against the altar. Then he took the*

> *book of the covenant, and read it in the hearing of the people;*
> *and they said, "All that the LORD has spoken we will do, and*
> *we will be obedient." Moses took the blood and dashed it on*
> *the people, and said, "See the blood of the covenant that the*
> *LORD has made with you in accordance with all these words."*
> *(Exod. 24:3–8)*

Question for Consideration

1. How do these ancient laws possibly affect today's society?

Sadly, we learn that Moses and Aaron will not make it to the land of Canaan. However, Moses demonstrates the depth of his leadership by attempting to make sure that his people are ready to embrace and deal with what is about to happen to them. In the book of Deuteronomy, Moses reminds the Israelites who their god is, where they are going, and their duties and responsibilities.

Deuteronomy 1–4: The first section revisits the Israelites' 40 years in the wilderness that have brought them to this point.
Deuteronomy 4–28: The second section reminds them that they must follow the laws Yahweh has given him and what will happen to them if they do not.
Deuteronomy 29–30: The third section explains that if the Israelites happen to mess up, they can repent and be restored.
Deuteronomy 31–34: In the final part of the book, Joshua is presented as the new Moses.

> *Then Moses summoned Joshua and said to him in the sight of*
> *all Israel: "Be strong and bold, for you are the one who will go*
> *with this people into the land that the LORD has sworn to their*
> *ancestors to give them; and you will put them in possession of*
> *it. [8] It is the LORD who goes before you. He will be with you; he*
> *will not fail you or forsake you. Do not fear or be dismayed"*
> *(Deut 31:7)*

Moses dies. In his honor, the writers also include two poems, the Song of Moses and the Blessing of Moses.

TABLE 5.2   Brief Outline of the Book of Joshua

The Conquests	1:1–12:24
Allotment of the Land of Canaan	13:1–24:33

Conquest of the Canaan

The Israelites and other ancient Near Eastern groups employ what is called a *cherem/kherem/herem* to initiate and justify their actions against another people. A *cherem* is defined, for the most part, as the total destruction of a group of people, their goods, and their possessions at the discretion and direction of the god or gods. This is the precedent and foundation set for the destruction of all peoples occupying Canaan. The biblical writers share that there were many groups living in the space at the time—Perizzites, Girgashites, Hivites, and others. Although it appears that they had all been living in the land for some time, Yahweh decreed that the groups were unfit to occupy this space and set to be driven out in the form of a *cherem* (genocide). They were occupying a space "promised" to the Israelites.

After a study of the land and a visit to a Canaanite brothel, Israelite spies report back what they are about to encounter. With this information, they work to develop a sound military strategy: hit the central part of the country, then go south, and finally move north. Once the plan has been established, Joshua leads the troops on the purging campaign of Canaan. First on the list is the capital city of Jericho.

The Israelites take the city of Jericho in a unique manner, using persistence, sound, and traditional warfare.

> On the seventh day they rose early, at the dawn of day, and marched around the city in the same manner seven times. It was only on that day that they marched around the city seven times. And at the seventh time, when the priests had blown the trumpets, Joshua said to the people, "Shout, for the LORD has given you the city. And the city and all that is within it shall be devoted to the LORD for destruction. Only Rahab the prostitute and all who are with her in her house shall live, because she hid the messengers whom we sent. But you, keep yourselves from the things devoted to destruction, lest when you have devoted them you take any of the devoted things and make the camp of Israel a thing for destruction and bring trouble upon it. But all silver and gold, and every vessel of bronze and iron, are holy to the LORD; they shall go into the treasury of the LORD." So the people shouted, and the trumpets were blown. As soon as the people heard the sound of the trumpet, the people shouted a great shout, and the wall fell down flat, so that the people went up into the city, every man straight before him, and they captured the city. Then they devoted all in the city to destruction, both men and women, young and old, oxen, sheep, and donkeys, with the edge of the sword. (Josh. 6:15–20)

The biblical writers describe a spectacular sight that resulted in a tremendous victory for the Israelites. Archaeologists have shared that the area labeled Jericho (a.k.a. Tell-es-Sultan) has been in existence since as early as 10,000 BCE, with various groups settling and thriving there. During the conquest of Jericho, during the Late Bronze Age (1500–1200 BCE), the biblical text states that Jericho was surrounded by a massive wall. Jericho's wall has been the subject of legendary folklore and the subject matter of songs:

> Joshua fit the battle of Jericho
> Jericho Jericho
> Joshua fit the battle of Jericho
> And the walls come tumbling down
> (African-American Spiritual)

After the great success at Jericho, they continue their battle for Canaan. However, they suffer a humiliating defeat from the tiny town of Ai.

> But the Israelites broke faith in regard to the devoted things: Achan son of Carmi son of Zabdi son of Zerah, of the tribe of Judah, took some of the devoted things; and the anger of the LORD burned against the Israelites. Joshua sent men from Jericho to Ai, which is near Beth-aven, east of Bethel, and said to them, "Go up and spy out the land." And the men went up and spied out Ai. Then they returned to Joshua and said to him, "Not all the people need go up; about two or three thousand men should go up and attack Ai. Since they are so few, do not make the whole people toil up there. So about three thousand of the people went up there; and they fled before the men of Ai. The men of Ai killed about thirty-six of them, chasing them from outside the gate as far as Shebarim and killing them on the slope. The hearts of the people melted and turned to water. (Josh. 7:1–5)

Even after their embarrassment, the Israelites go on to be successful in their quest, conquering sixteen cities. The book of Joshua concludes with the Israelites conquering the land of Canaan, just as it was told to Moses.

> So Joshua took the whole land, according to all that the LORD had spoken to Moses. (Josh. 11:23)

This seems to bring the story to a nice, near end, yet in the following book, Judges, the Israelites are still fighting people in Canaan.

> *After the death of Joshua, the people of Israel inquired of the*
> *LORD, "Who shall go up first for us against the Canaanites, to*
> *fight against them?" (Judg. 1:1)*

If they subdued the whole land at the end of Joshua, why are they still fighting? This question has motivated scholars to explore how Israel actually comes into the land of Canaan. Investigation of this theory has generated a plethora of additional questions and theories regarding what happened. Following are four that present different perspectives.

Conquest Model

This model argues that the Israelites came to occupy Canaan as the Bible states (Josh. 1–12). The military strategy presented by Joshua states that they entered the central highlands, went south conquering cities in that region, then went north to finish the job. Scholars who have supported this theory include: William Foxwell Albright, G. Ernst Wright, John Bright, Yigal Yadin, and Abraham Malamat.

Although the writers' presentation of this conquest is exciting, it has some major difficulties. Chiefly, physical evidence doesn't support this theory. Because the city of Jericho has unquestionably been identified and excavated for decades, one would expect to find some remains or evidence of battle. The taking of Jericho would date to approximately the twelfth century BCE. However, archaeological excavations have revealed that at this level, the city had only a few people living there. Remains of a wall date to 1000 years earlier, and there is another wall and tower that date to the Neolithic period (8500–4300 BCE). This is, of course, well before the event described by biblical writers. The site of Ai has been located as well, but there was no large population dating to the 12th century.

> *It is a sad fact that of the town walls of the Late Bronze Age,*
> *within which period the attack by the Israelites must fall by*
> *any dating, not a trace remains....The excavation of Jericho,*
> *therefore, has thrown no light on the walls of Jericho of which*
> *the destruction is so vividly described in the Book of Joshua.[3]*

Moreover, the writers explain that 16 cities were destroyed. While three—Lachish, Bethel, and Hazor—have some evidence of conflagration, it is extremely difficult to connect them with the Israelite invasion. The destruction may have been the result of battles with other groups in the region. The other cities have not yet been located or do not show any evidence of destruction that links clearly with Israelite warfare.

---

3   Kathleen Kenyon, *Digging Up Jericho* (London: Ernest Benn 1957, 261-2).

The Peaceful Infiltration Model/German Approach

This theory offers that there was no large military conflict as described by the biblical writers. If there was any such warfare, it would have been during the transition from the system of judges to the monarchy. However, archaeology does not support this thought either. Scholars Martin Noth and Albrect Alt assert that what we come to know as Israel were seminomadic clans that migrated and settled in various places next to those groups that were stabilized and sedentary in the region. There is evidence of a number of unfortified village sites (75–125 people) in the area. It's not clear why these groups moved into the area. It is possible that some may have been fleeing or avoiding the influx of groups of Sea Peoples (e.g., Philistines, Denyen, Tjeker, etc.) moving into the region, but this is not conclusive. Nevertheless, interaction (e.g., trade, politics) between groups would have generated changes in settlement patterns, how people lived, and other cultural activities. A new or different culture may have developed out of this kind of interplay and created what came to be known as Israel.

Emergence of Early Israel: R. B. Coote's Model

Scholar Robert Coote argues that early Israel/Palestine developed within itself. While Egypt was the imperialistic power at the time, Coote presents the idea of a division between the elite and masses. Like all ruling powers, Egyptian fell into decline. In order to compensate for its developing issues, Egypt focused its energies on military activities and Egyptian administrators and governors. These actions affected the region of Israel/Palestine—a decrease in the Israelite population and Egyptian settlements. Eventually, the Philistines made their way into the area and challenged the Egyptians and overtook them during the Egyptian decline. The Philistines gained a stronghold in the lowlands of Israel/Palestine, which pushed the elites into the highlands. Coote suggests that the Israel described by the biblical writers developed primarily as a result of the Egyptian issues and eventual decline, and the entrance of the Philistines. He also offers that with Israel's development, the man we know as David would have emerged as leader, a tribal sheik, who governed the central and northern highlands, and unified the low and highlands.[4]

Peasant Revolt Model

Our final theory suggests that there was in fact a revolt against the imperialistic power of the time. During this time, the most dominant force in the region was Egypt. There were Egyptian garrisons established in Canaan. However, there were also Canaanite city-state leaders that ruled Canaan as well (think about counties within in a state or countries within a nation). Most of them reported in some fashion to the Egyptian establishment. George Mendenhall and Norman Gottwald theorized that those oppressed by the Canaanite city-state leaders revolted. They would have been oppressed with heavy taxes, forced labor, and control over the goods they produced. This model reflects aspects of Marxist theory, as it describes the underclass galvanizing to overthrow its tyrannous rulers.

---

4   Robert B. Coote. "Early Israel," Scandinavian *Journal of the Old Testament 2*. (1991): 35–46.

Mendenhall and Gottwald agree on everything except the impetus for the revolt. Mendenhall states that Yahweh is viewed as a liberator, which sparks the revolt. Gottwald argues that the people revolted because of the mistreatment, and Yahweh was incorporated later. Although the Peasant Revolt idea works well within the political climate and issues known at this time, there is no archaeological evidence to support this theory either.

Allotment of Land and Covenant Renewal

The book of Joshua ends with the division of the conquered land of Canaan. Most of the groups settle within the area, but the tribes of Reuben, Gad, and the half-tribe of Manasseh will reside in Gilead, just east of the Jordan River (Josh. 13:8–32). The Levites are special, however. They do not receive any land but instead are charged with the critical priestly duties for Israel (e.g., overseeing the Ark of the Covenant). In return for their service, they receive part of the tithe (Num. 18:21–26).

After the allotment of the land is complete, Joshua calls the people together, and they revisit the covenant ceremony previously instituted by Moses as they prepared to enter Canaan. Joshua, like Moses, reminds the people who is their god, what the deity has done for them, what they owe in return, and that they should avoid at all cost serving other deities.

STUDY QUESTIONS

1. How are Joshua and Moses similar to each other?
2. How do they differ?
3. How do you define the term cherem?
4. What would be the purpose(s) of a cherem?
5. Was the Israelite invasion of Canaan justified? Why or why not?

TABLE 5.3 Judges

Continuing conquest of the land	1:1–2:20
Stories of varying length about individual judges	2:11–16:31
Two stories about intertribal conflict	17–21

Brief Outline of Judges

Following the exodus from Egypt and the 40-year wilderness journey, the Israelites established themselves in what we know as the land of Canaan. Debates remain regarding how they entered the land, but whatever the case, Canaan is eventually taken over and becomes Israel. Remember,

Moses never made it into Canaan and has passed away. His replacement, Joshua, has also died. So how will Israel be governed now that their leaders are gone? Yahweh will raise up judges.

Judges and the judicial system are part of our everyday lives. Judges preside in courtrooms where life-changing decisions are made. Judges mediate disputes. They determine laws that shape culture and affect how people interact with each other. Judges help to establish and implement penal codes. At some point in our lives, many of us will or have encountered judges, or our lives are or will be affected by their decisions.

In Israel, Yahweh raises up judges to govern the people of Israel. After the death of Joshua, the people of Israel inquired of the LORD, "Who shall go up first for us against the Canaanites, to fight against them?" (Judg. 1:1).

As a result of Yahweh's decision, Israel now has individual judges who will help to govern Israel. Note that Israel still remains a theocracy:

> *Yahweh is king;*
> *Yahweh raises up judges;*
> *the judges govern Yahweh's people.*

Think about ancient Israelite judges and modern judges. What commonalities do they have?

The stories about judges that have been collected and compiled share topics including but not limited to warfare, family, and love. Like most of the Bible, the stories more than likely come from oral traditions that were eventually written down. There are some questions concerning how the stories and the tribes of Israel relate to each other. It appears that there may be at least two valid ways to view the relationship between them.

First school of thought: Tribes have a conscious unity; essentially what the Bible presents. The general idea is that there was a succession of leaders/judges who ruled a united Israel from the death of Joshua to the monarchy.

Second of school of thought: Tribes were independent, with an evolving sense of unity. Initially, no conscious unity; stories reflect separate interests and identities of the tribes that later became Israel.

List of Israelite Judges and some of their characteristics:

> *Othniel (Judg. 3:9): deliverer*
> *Ehud (Judg. 3:12–30): left-handed*
> *Shamgar (Judg. 3:31): beats group with an ox goad*
> *Deborah (Judg. 4–5): only female judge; renaissance woman*
> *Gideon (Judg. 6–8): trickster*
> *Abimelech (Judg. 9:26–41) warrior*
> *Tola (Judg. 10:1–2): no recorded deeds*
> *Jair (Judg. 10:3–5): controlled 23 cities in Gilead*

Jephthah (Judg. 11–12): warrior
Ibzan (Judg. 12:8–10): no recorded deeds
Elon (Judg. 12:11): n.o recorded deeds
Abdon (Judg. 12:13–15): no recorded deeds
Samson (Judg. 13–16): nazirite; the most well-known judge of
ancient Israel. He is superhero-like with his enormous strength.
He is cunning, cocky, and a nemesis to the Philistines. He
outsmarts them; however, they eventually capture and blind
him. Yet Samson manages to summon enough of his power to
destroy a huge number of them before his demise.
Eli (1 Sam. 1:1–4:22): also a priest
Samuel (1 Sam. 7:15): nazirite

The Final Section of Judges

The book of Judges ends with two intense stories. The first shares the origin of the Danite priesthood. Micah, an Ephraimite, makes sacred objects and hires a Levite to oversee them and his house. A group of Danites persuade the Levite to join them and take Micah's objects with them. The Danites conquer the area of Laish, which becomes Dan.

The second is a gruesome story about another Levite and his concubine. The concubine is gang raped, tortured, and killed by men of the tribe of Benjamin. The Levite then cuts the body into twelve pieces and sends one to each tribe. This act incites a civil war in which the tribes go after and defeat Benjamin. They vow not to intermarry with Benjamites but end up providing wives for them without breaking the oath. Judges ends with a phrase that told the fate of the Israelites on a number of occasions and suggests that a change is on the horizon for them:

> *In those days there was no king in Israel. Everyone did what was*
> *right in his own eyes. (Judg. 21:25)*

Credits

CHAPTER 6

Move to Kingship

Early Monarchic Period (1050–930 BCE)

Israelite culture now begins a momentous shift. The days of judges are coming to an end. Corruption, deceit, theft, and disregard of priestly traditions are running rampant, as well as ideas of what a leader should be. The people feel a change is necessary and make demands for it to happen.

Samuel unknowingly helps usher in the monarchy. Much like Isaac, Jacob, Samson, and others, Samuel enters the story via a barren motif. Elkanah has two wives, Peninah and Hannah. Peninah has a child; Hannah does not and has been labeled as barren. Remember that a number of the children born to such "barren" mothers are often special or go on to do something exceptional. Because Hannah desires to give birth to a son, she goes up to the shrine at Shiloh and makes a vow to Yahweh. Hannah promises that if she is blessed with a son, she will make sure that he is a nazirite (an individual made special to serve the deity [Yahweh]; they often have specific vows to maintain, such as not cutting one's hair, refraining from alcohol, etc.):

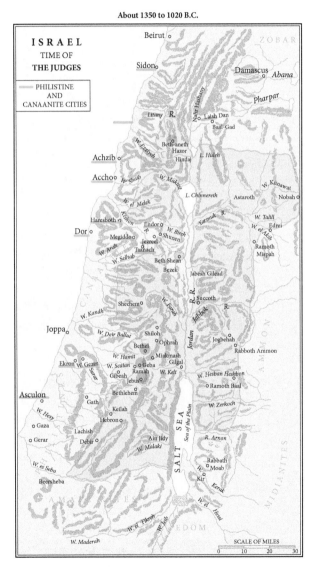

FIG. 6.1 **Map of Israel during the Period of Judges**

TABLE 6.1 Brief Outline of Books of Samuel

Story of Samuel—move from Judges to kingship/monarchy	1 Sam. 1–7
Story of Saul—Israel's first king can be two sections:	1 Sam. 8–31
Samuel and Saul	1 Sam. 8–15
Saul and David	1 Sam. 16–31
Rise of David	2 Sam. 1–10
Court History	2 Sam. 11–20
Appendices	2 Sam. 21–24

And she vowed a vow and said, "O LORD of hosts, if you will indeed look on the affliction of your servant and remember me and not forget your servant, but will give to your servant a son, then I will give him to the LORD all the days of his life, and no razor shall touch his head.' (1 Sam. 1:11)

While there, Eli, who is in charge, sees Hannah moving her lips, but there is no sound. He presumes that she is drunk. However, he learns that she is praying fervently. Hannah gives birth to Samuel. The writers explain that she has other children as well.

Indeed the LORD visited Hannah, and she conceived and bore three sons and two daughters (1 Sam. 2:21).

To fulfill her vow to Yahweh, Hannah takes Samuel to Shiloh once he's weaned. He adheres to his nazirite vows and remains at Shiloh with Eli, learning the priestly duties. It is here that we see the prophetic call of Samuel.

At that time Eli, whose eyesight had begun to grow dim so that he could not see, was lying down in his own place. The lamp of God had not yet gone out, and Samuel was lying down in the temple of the LORD, where the ark of God was. Then the LORD called Samuel, and he said, "Here I am!" and ran to Eli and said, "Here I am, for you called me." But he said, "I did not call; lie down again." So he went and lay down. And the LORD called again, "Samuel!" and Samuel arose and went to Eli and said, "Here I am, for you called me." But he said, "I did not call, my son; lie down again." Now Samuel did not yet know the LORD, and the word of the LORD had not yet been revealed to him. And the LORD called Samuel again the third time. And he arose and went to Eli and said, "Here I am, for you called me." Then Eli perceived that the LORD was calling the boy. Therefore Eli said to Samuel, "Go, lie down, and if he calls you, you shall say, 'Speak, LORD, for your servant hears.'" So Samuel went and lay down in his place. (1 Sam. 3:2–9)

Eli's sons were also priests, but they were extremely corrupt. A man comes to visit Eli to discuss this problem and explain what will happen as a result.

"Why then do you scorn my sacrifices and my offerings that I commanded for my dwelling, and honor your sons above me by fattening yourselves on the choicest parts of every offering of my people Israel?" Therefore the LORD, the God of Israel, declares: "I promised that your house and the house of your father should go in and out before me forever," but now the LORD declares: "Far be it from me, for those who honor me I will honor, and those who despise me shall be lightly esteemed. Behold, the days are coming when I will cut off your strength and the strength of your father's house, so that there will not be an old man in your house. Then in distress you will look with envious eye on all the prosperity that shall be bestowed on Israel, and there shall not be an old man in your house forever. The only one of you whom I shall not cut off from my altar shall be spared to weep his eyes out to grieve his heart, and all the descendants of your house shall die by the sword of men. And this that shall come upon your two sons, Hophni and Phinehas, shall be the sign to you: both of them shall die on the same day." (1 Sam. 2:29–34)

Dismissal of Samuel

Samuel was an incredible judge, warrior, and renaissance man in Israel. Under his leadership, the Philistines, who were a major opponent of the Israelites, were subdued. Israel and its people thrived under his direction. He sons, Joel and Abijah, two of the last judges in Israel, were a different story, however. Like the sons of Eli, Hophni and Phinehas, Samuel's sons were also corrupt. They also robbed the people and improperly administered sacrifices.

When Samuel became old, he made his sons judges over Israel. The name of his firstborn son was Joel, and the name of his second, Abijah; they were judges in Beersheba. Yet his sons did not walk in his ways but turned aside after gain. They took bribes and perverted justice. (1 Sam. 8:1–3)

The people of Israel were disturbed by this pattern of behavior, and to make matters worse, the one shining judicial light, Samuel, was aging. Even in antiquity, age was at times a factor in some aspects of Israelite life (e.g., childbirth, leadership), and some may argue it as a form of discrimination. Samuel had served Israel mightily. Although his sons were the antithesis of how he approached governing Israel, Samuel did everything he could to be effective. He was a true monotheist—following Yahweh and Yahweh only. Nevertheless, the people were tired of his sons' behavior, and they felt that Samuel was now too old for the job. As a matter of fact, they wanted a change not only in leadership but in the type of leadership. They wanted a king. Israel wanted a flesh and blood figure; one who was tangible. Every nation around them had a monarch. It was time for them to have one, and they made their desire known to Samuel. Moreover, they instructed Samuel to go to Yahweh with their petition and complaint.

Samuel reluctantly did as instructed. As expected, he felt rejected. After all the work he had done for his people, this is what it had come to. But Yahweh helped to alleviate his concerns. Yahweh explained that the people were rejecting him and not Samuel.

> *Then all the elders of Israel gathered together and came to Samuel at Ramah and said to him, "Behold, you are old and your sons do not walk in your ways. Now appoint for us a king to judge us like all the nations." But the thing displeased Samuel when they said, "Give us a king to judge us." And Samuel prayed to the LORD. And the LORD said to Samuel, "Obey the voice of the people in all that they say to you, for they have not rejected you, but they have rejected me from being king over them. According to all the deeds that they have done, from the day I brought them up out of Egypt even to this day, forsaking me and serving other gods, so they are also doing to you. Now then, obey their voice; only you shall solemnly warn them and show them the ways of the king who shall reign over them." (1 Sam. 8:4–9)*

Yahweh tells Samuel that he will give the people what they desire, but the deity also tells him to explain to them what will happen once they receive their king.

> *So Samuel told all the words of the LORD to the people who were asking for a king from him. He said, "These will be the ways of the king who will reign over you: he will take your sons and appoint them to his chariots and to be his horsemen and to run before his chariots. And he will appoint for himself commanders of thousands and commanders of fifties, and some to plow his ground and to reap his harvest, and to make his implements of war and the equipment of his chariots. He will take your*

daughters to be perfumers and cooks and bakers. He will take the best of your fields and vineyards and olive orchards and give them to his servants. He will take the tenth of your grain and of your vineyards and give it to his officers and to his servants. He will take your male servants and female servants and the best of your young men, and your donkeys, and put them to his work. He will take the tenth of your flocks, and you shall be his slaves. And in that day you will cry out because of your king, whom you have chosen for yourselves, but the LORD will not answer you in that day." (1 Sam. 8:10–18)

This act sets the stage for the beginning of the monarchy. Like the enigmatic emergence of Israel into the land of Canaan, there are two parts of a unique theory for the rise of the monarchy:

The Traditional/Complex Model

This model proposes that the monarchy was forced on Israel by external pressures; it was brought about by well-planned policy. The Israelites existed in small tribal units led by the tribes' elders but had developed a system of charismatic leadership for war. Under normal circumstances, they could handle the usual threats (e.g., skirmishes and disagreements between families or tribes). This aspect of the theory sees the Philistines as part of the necessity for a king. The Philistines presented a different type of threat compared to the typical local threats. This group of the Sea Peoples were armed and well-trained and came in significant numbers. Theirs was a united front in religious, political, and economic terms. The Philistines gained victories in the center of the hill country, while others—Ammonites and Amalekites—began to cause Israel troubles on their flanks. Thus, strong, centralized power and leadership were necessary to handle this level of threat to Israel. Saul was the man, and the central region of the country was the place because conflicts were taking place there. After Saul defeated the Ammonites in his initial encounter when he became king, the people realized that he could be their permanent charismatic leader.

According to this model, several factors came together in the Iron Age period (1200–1000 BCE) that led to the development of the kingdom; to reduce the issue to one factor is to concentrate on only one component of a complex issue. To say that the conflict with the Philistines brought about the need for a king is to make a necessary component into the sufficient and sole element. An expanding population led to the establishment of villages in an ever-growing geographic range. This growth led to increased contact with neighboring groups, which would develop relationships that could be beneficial or contentious. The people may need to be protected. For example, increase and specialization in the area of food and animal production led to trade between different groups and peoples. These kinds of trade relationships would need to be protected and monitored.

Saul Arrives on the Scene

Saul enters the picture. Consider how he is characterized and described in his progression toward the kingship.

> *There was a man of Benjamin whose name was Kish son of Abiel son of Zeror son of Becorath son of Aphiah, a Benjaminite, a man of wealth. He had a son whose name was Saul, a handsome young man. There was not a man among the people of Israel more handsome than he; he stood head and shoulders above everyone else.* (1 Sam. 9:1–2)

The writers present Saul as:

- handsome
- head and shoulders above everyone else (tall)
- a Benjamite (least of all the tribes); per Saul, his family is also the humblest of that tribe

> *Saul answered, "I am only a Benjaminite, from the least of the tribes of Israel, and my family is the humblest of all the families of the tribe of Benjamin."* (1 Sam 9:21)

Yahweh approves Saul to Samuel. This is an important aspect of the story. Keep in mind that although the people request a king, they do not get to choose who this will be. Yahweh, the divine king they rejected, does this.

> *Now the day before Saul came, the LORD had revealed to Samuel: "Tomorrow about this time I will send to you a man from the land of Benjamin, and you shall anoint him to be ruler over my people Israel. He shall save my people from the hand of the Philistines; for I have seen the suffering of my people, because their outcry has come to me." When Samuel saw Saul, the LORD told him, "Here is the man of whom I spoke to you. He it is who shall rule over my people."* (1 Sam. 9:15–17)

We learn that Saul is looking for his father's donkeys. The animals had strayed, and Kish told his son to take one of his boys and go find them. They had no luck. Saul is advised to go and visit the man of Yahweh, as he may be of some help. They share a meal and spend time conversing. Samuel eventually explains to Saul that he has a message from Yahweh that he needs to make known to him.

> *Samuel took a vial of oil and poured it on his head, and kissed him; he said, "The LORD has anointed you ruler over his people Israel. You shall reign over the people of the LORD and you will save them from the hand of their enemies all around. Now this shall be the sign to you that the LORD has anointed you ruler over his heritage. (1 Sam. 10:1)*

Saul's anointing by Samuel initiates the monarchy in Israel. Israel has its first king.

It takes some time for the kingship to take effect. A while after the anointing, Saul led a successful battle against the Ammonites.

> *The next day Saul put the people in three companies. At the morning watch they came into the camp and cut down the Ammonites until the heat of the day; and those who survived were scattered, so that no two of them were left together. (1 Sam. 11:11)*

Saul officially becomes king of Israel, finally being crowned at Gilgal.

After some successes in his reign, Saul begins to have issues. Remember, he is the first one to do this. There is no blueprint, no guidebook. What does it mean to be king of Israel, this newly formed group? It could be argued that Saul was more of a chief than what was understood as a traditional king. They are transitioning from a tribal, chiefdom system of judges. How are the newly anointed king and the kingship supposed to function? Does the king ever function as a priest? What are the limits of the king's power over the people? Is the king Yahweh's representative?

Like anyone in a new job or position, Saul makes mistakes. Although he has been successful as a military leader, he doesn't have a true professional army, especially when compared to the surrounding powers in the ancient Near East. There are also some concerns regarding nepotism. For instance, his son Jonathan is one of his leading officers.

Saul encounters a conflict with some of the intricacies in warfare and ritual. While preparing for an impending battle with the Philistines, Saul and his troops are instructed to wait for Samuel, who is to arrive there before the clash starts. They are to participate in a ceremonial sacrifice that Samuel is to preside over. Samuel is late, so Saul decides to proceed with the oblation. Just as he finishes, Samuel arrives and discovers what Saul has done. He tells Saul that he has blown it to remain king over Israel because he did not follow instructions given by Yahweh. Thus, Saul's kingdom will come to an end.

> *Samuel said to Saul, "You have done foolishly; you have not kept the commandment of the LORD your God, which he commanded you. The LORD would have established your*

*kingdom over Israel forever, but now your kingdom will not
continue; the LORD has sought out a man after his own heart;
and the LORD has appointed him to be ruler over his people,
because you have not kept what the LORD commanded you."
(1 Sam. 13:13–14)*

The authority of prophet versus king also comes to the forefront in an impending conflict with the Amalekites. The Israelites were instructed to institute a *cherem* against the Amalekites. In this particular *cherem*, they were to annihilate the Amalekites—leave nothing alive. Saul took it upon himself to alter the instructions and leave the Amalekite king, Agag, alive. He also decided to keep part of their herds. When Samuel learns what Saul has done, he is furious.

*But Samuel said, "What then is this bleating of sheep in my ears,
and the lowing of cattle that I hear?" (1 Sam. 15:14)*

When Samuel questions Saul and what he's done, he retorts with a weak attempt to justify his action.

*Saul said, "They have brought them from the Amalekites; for the
people spared the best of the sheep and the cattle, to sacrifice
to the LORD your God; but the rest we have utterly destroyed."
(1 Sam. 15:15)*

*"I have obeyed the voice of the LORD, I have gone on the mission
on which the LORD sent me, I have brought Agag the king of
Amalek, and I have utterly destroyed the Amalekites. But from
the spoil the people took sheep and cattle, the best of the things
devoted to destruction, to sacrifice to the LORD your God in
Gilgal." (1 Sam. 15:20-21)*

Thus, Samuel announces Saul's demise again.

*"For rebellion is no less a sin than divination, and stubbornness
is like iniquity and idolatry. Because you have rejected the word
of the LORD, he has also rejected you from being king." (1 Sam.
15:23)*

It was downhill from here for Saul. Yahweh was upset at his new king and his actions. The writers explain that Yahweh regretted that he had made him king (1 Sam 15:11).

1. Whom among all the characters in the story do you think the narrator supports? Why?

2. What do you think about the relationship between Samuel and Saul? Is it amicable? Do they hate each other? Do they have anything in common?

3. Is there anything in the narrative that suggests that the attitude toward the monarchy was not always positive? If so, why do you think this was so?

David Makes His Appearance

Samuel stated on at least two occasions that because of the things Saul has done, he will no longer remain king. Yahweh's regret of even selecting Saul solidifies Samuel's proclamation. Samuel's declaration transpires, but on a somewhat dishonorable, lengthy path to Saul's demise. Because Saul is essentially a lame duck, Yahweh and Samuel make moves to bring in the next king for the burgeoning monarchy.

Yahweh instructs Samuel to approach Jesse the Bethlehemite. It is from his sons that the next king of Israel will come.

> Jesse made seven of his sons pass before Samuel, and Samuel said to Jesse, "The LORD has not chosen any of these." Samuel said to Jesse, "Are all your sons here?" And he said, "There remains yet the youngest, but he is keeping the sheep." And Samuel said to Jesse, "Send and bring him; for we will not sit down until he comes here." He sent and brought him in. Now, he was ruddy, and had beautiful eyes, and was handsome. The LORD said, "Rise and anoint him; for this is the one." Then Samuel took the horn of oil, and anointed him in the presence of his brothers; and the spirit of the LORD came mightily upon David from that day forward. Samuel then set out and went to Ramah. (1 Sam.16:10–13)

David, like Saul, was introduced with specific characteristics that are similar but also specific to him:

- ruddy
- beautiful eyes
- handsome
- skilled lyre player

- warrior
- skilled at speech
- man of valor
- a man good in presence

Like Samuel, he is also a renaissance man. The rise of David, the younger brother, from lowly shepherd to king of Israel is reminiscent of Joseph, also a younger brother, in the Genesis story.

David's ascension to power is intriguing and a masterful, meandering story. After being chosen by Yahweh and anointed by Samuel, David enters King Saul's court as an adept musician to comfort the king in his psychotic illnesses.

> Now the spirit of the LORD departed from Saul, and an evil spirit from the LORD tormented him. And Saul's servants said to him, "See now, an evil spirit from God is tormenting you. Let our lord now command the servants who attend you to look for someone who is skillful in playing the lyre; and when the evil spirit from God is upon you, he will play it, and you will feel better." So Saul said to his servants, "Provide for me someone who can play well, and bring him to me." One of the young men answered, "I have seen a son of Jesse the Bethlehemite who is skillful in playing, a man of valor, a warrior, prudent in speech, and a man of good presence; and the LORD is with him." So Saul sent messengers to Jesse, and said, "Send me your son David who is with the sheep." Jesse took a donkey loaded with bread, a skin of wine, and a kid, and sent them by his son David to Saul. And David came to Saul, and entered his service. Saul loved him greatly, and he became his armor-bearer. Saul sent to Jesse, saying, "Let David remain in my service, for he has found favor in my sight." And whenever the evil spirit from God came upon Saul, David took the lyre and played it with his hand, and Saul would be relieved and feel better, and the evil spirit would depart from him. (1 Sam. 16:14–23)

He also shows his worth as a warrior by defeating the giant Philistine soldier, Goliath.

> When the Philistine drew nearer to meet David, David ran quickly toward the battle line to meet the Philistine. David put his hand in his bag, took out a stone, slung it, and struck the Philistine on his forehead; the stone sank into his forehead, and he fell face down on the ground. So David prevailed over the Philistine

> *with a sling and a stone, striking down the Philistine and killing*
> *him; there was no sword in David's hand. Then David ran and*
> *stood over the Philistine; he grasped his sword, drew it out of*
> *its sheath, and killed him; then he cut off his head with it. When*
> *the Philistines saw that their champion was dead, they fled.*
> *(1 Sam. 17:48–51)*

Note that later in the books of Samuel, a figure named Elhanan is also credited with killing Goliath.

> *Then there was another battle with the Philistines at Gob; and*
> *Elhanan son of Jaare-oregim, the Bethlehemite, killed Goliath*
> *the Gittite, the shaft of whose spear was like a weaver's beam.*
> *(2 Sam. 21:19)*

David also marries Saul's daughter, Michal.

> *Then Saul said to David, "Here is my elder daughter Merab; I*
> *will give her to you as a wife. Only be valiant for me and fight*
> *the LORD's battles." For Saul thought, "Let not my hand be*
> *against him, but let the hand of the Philistines be against him."*
> *(1 Sam. 18:17);*

> *Now Saul's daughter Michal loved David. Saul was told, and the*
> *thing pleased him. (1 Sam. 18:20)*

And he and Jonathan, Saul's son, become best friends.

> *When David had finished speaking to Saul, the soul of Jonathan*
> *was bound to the soul of David, and Jonathan loved him as his*
> *own soul. Saul took him that day and would not let him return to*
> *his father's house. Then Jonathan made a covenant with David,*
> *because he loved him as his own soul. Jonathan stripped himself*
> *of the robe that he was wearing, and gave it to David, and his*
> *armor, and even his sword and his bow and his belt (1 Sam. 18:1–4)*

David is deeply entrenched in Saul's family and within the king's court. A close reading of these events reveals that they are anachronistic, which may lend more credence to the Documentary Hypothesis discussed in chapter two and the combining of different stories about David, Saul, and events in which they were involved.

As David's popularity grows, so does Saul's jealousy.

> *As they were coming home, when David returned from killing the Philistine, the women came out of all the towns of Israel, singing and dancing, to meet King Saul, with tambourines, with songs of joy, and with musical instruments. And the women sang to one another as they made merry, "Saul has killed his thousands, and David his ten thousands." (1 Sam. 18:6–7).*

The zenith of Saul's envy hits while David is performing for Saul. David realizes that he will soon have to leave in order to save his life.

> *The next day an evil spirit from God rushed upon Saul, and he raved within his house, while David was playing the lyre, as he did day by day. Saul had his spear in his hand; and Saul threw the spear, for he thought, "I will pin David to the wall." But David eluded him twice. (1 Sam. 18:10–11)*

Michal and Jonathan understand this as well and help David escape. Michal puts a *teraphim* (understood to be a kind of household statute of a deity; also this appears to be both the singular and plural form of the word) in David's bed to make it appear to the guards that David was in bed.

David is now on the run, carefully managing a complex cat-and-mouse game between him and Saul. During his journey, he builds relationships with some allies (e.g., elders, Achish, Abiathar); he also marries Abigail and Ahinoam. Many of these relationships will benefit him as his kingdom develops.

There are, however, those that have conflict with David. Nabal refuses to provide David's troops with supplies. His wife, Abigail, intervenes and gives David the supplies. After Nabal gets drunk at a party, he dies from a sudden heart issue. Shortly after, David marries Abigail.

The chase continues during the decline of Saul's reign. Why doesn't David put an end to this and just kill Saul? He has two opportunities to do this with ease, but he doesn't. In one instance, David is hiding in a cave in En-gedi while Saul relieves himself.

> *When Saul returned from following the Philistines, he was told, "David is in the wilderness of En-gedi." Then Saul took three thousand chosen men out of all Israel, and went to look for David and his men in the direction of the Rocks of the Wild Goats. He came to the sheepfolds beside the road, where there was a cave; and Saul went in to relieve himself. Now David and his men were sitting in the innermost parts of the cave. The men of David said to him, "Here is the day of which the LORD said*

> *to you, 'I will give your enemy into your hand, and you shall do to him as it seems good to you.'" Then David went and stealthily cut off a corner of Saul's cloak. Afterward David was stricken to the heart because he had cut off a corner of Saul's cloak. He said to his men, "The LORD forbid that I should do this thing to my lord, the LORD's anointed, to raise my hand against him; for he is the LORD's anointed." So David scolded his men severely and did not permit them to attack Saul. Then Saul got up and left the cave, and went on his way. (1 Sam. 24:1–7)*

In a second instance, David and his troops had Saul and his army surrounded. Abishai and David sneak up on Saul while he's sleeping. Abishai asks David for permission to stab Saul with a spear.

> *Then David said to Ahimelech the Hittite, and to Joab's brother Abishai son of Zeruiah, "Who will go down with me into the camp to Saul?" Abishai said, "I will go down with you." So David and Abishai went to the army by night; there Saul lay sleeping within the encampment, with his spear stuck in the ground at his head; and Abner and the army lay around him. Abishai said to David, "God has given your enemy into your hand today; now therefore let me pin him to the ground with one stroke of the spear; I will not strike him twice." (1 Sam. 26:6–8)*

Why won't David let this happen? No matter what Saul has done or continues to do, David understands that Saul is Yahweh's anointed and must not be harmed.

Before David officially becomes king of Israel, he works as a mercenary. The Philistine king of Gath, Achish, gives him the city of Ziklag. In return, David uses his military prowess to assist the Philistines. All along, he is deceiving them for his benefit. His deception is reminiscent of trickster stories seen earlier, with other biblical figures.

> *Then David said to Achish, "If I have found favor in your sight, let a place be given me in one of the country towns, so that I may live there; for why should your servant live in the royal city with you?" So that day Achish gave him Ziklag; therefore Ziklag has belonged to the kings of Judah to this day. The length of time that David lived in the country of the Philistines was one year and four months. Now David and his men went up and made raids on the Geshurites, the Girzites, and the Amalekites; for these were the landed settlements from Telam on the way to*

Shur and on to the land of Egypt. David struck the land, leaving neither man nor woman alive, but took away the sheep, the oxen, the donkeys, the camels, and the clothing, and came back to Achish. When Achish asked, "Against whom have you made a raid today?" David would say, "Against the Negeb of Judah," or "Against the Negeb of the Jerahmeelites," or "Against the Negeb of the Kenites." David left neither man nor woman alive to be brought back to Gath, thinking, "They might tell about us, and say, 'David has done so and so.'" Such was his practice all the time he lived in the country of the Philistines. Achish trusted David, thinking, "He has made himself utterly abhorrent to his people Israel; therefore he shall always be my servant." (1 Sam. 27:5–12)

Saul becomes desperate, so much so that he goes against his own law regarding consulting mediums. He visits a woman who often bears the title the "witch" at Endor in a frantic attempt to speak with Samuel, who has by this time died.

Now Samuel had died, and all Israel had mourned for him and buried him in Ramah, his own city. Saul had expelled the mediums and the wizards from the land. (1 Sam.28:3)

So Saul disguised himself and put on other clothes and went there, he and two men with him. They came to the woman by night. And he said, "Consult a spirit for me, and bring up for me the one whom I name to you." The woman said to him, "Surely you know what Saul has done, how he has cut off the mediums and the wizards from the land. Why then are you laying a snare for my life to bring about my death?" But Saul swore to her by the LORD, "As the LORD lives, no punishment shall come upon you for this thing." Then the woman said, "Whom shall I bring up for you?" He answered, "Bring up Samuel for me." When the woman saw Samuel, she cried out with a loud voice; and the woman said to Saul, "Why have you deceived me? You are Saul!" The king said to her, "Have no fear; what do you see?" The woman said to Saul, "I see a divine being coming up out of the ground." He said to her, "What is his appearance?" She said, "An old man is coming up; he is wrapped in a robe." So Saul knew that it was Samuel, and he bowed with his face to the ground, and did obeisance. (1 Sam. 28:8–14)

Samuel reiterates his earlier message to Saul that the kingdom will be taken from him and given to David. He wants Saul to know that his efforts to prolong the inevitable are futile.

Saul's tragic end finally arrives. Just as Samuel told him, Saul and his sons are killed on the battlefield while fighting the Philistines at Gilboa.

> *Now the Philistines fought against Israel; and the men of Israel fled before the Philistines, and many fell on Mount Gilboa. The Philistines overtook Saul and his sons; and the Philistines killed Jonathan and Abinadab and Malchishua, the sons of Saul. The battle pressed hard upon Saul; the archers found him, and he was badly wounded by them. Then Saul said to his armor-bearer, "Draw your sword and thrust me through with it, so that these uncircumcised may not come and thrust me through, and make sport of me." But his armor-bearer was unwilling; for he was terrified. So Saul took his own sword and fell upon it. When his armor-bearer saw that Saul was dead, he also fell upon his sword and died with him. So Saul and his three sons and his armor-bearer and all his men died together on the same day.* (1 Sam. 31:1–6)

David expresses his grief and love for his family through a lament, "The Song of the Bow." Following is an excerpt:

> *Your glory, O Israel, lies slain upon your high places! How the mighty have fallen! Tell it not in Gath, proclaim it not in the streets of Ashkelon; or the daughters of the Philistines will rejoice, the daughters of the uncircumcised will exult.* (2 Sam. 2:19-20)

David comes to the throne officially and rules in Hebron in Judah for seven years. The transition was turbulent. Abner, Saul's uncle and general, put Saul's son Ishbaal (a.k.a. Ishbosheth) on the throne to rule the northern tribes. Conflict developed between David and Ishbaal over the seven years, but most of these appear to have been issues regarding the borders of the kingdoms. Family murders and dramas transpire as the Israelite kingdom takes shape:

- Joab (David's general) murders Abner.
- Ishbaal is murdered by his advisers.

The northern tribes now have no true leader, with the murder of Ishbaal. The closest is Mephibosheth, a grandson of Saul, son of Jonathan, who is physically challenged (2 Sam. 9). At the request of the elders, David becomes king of all Israel. At the age of 30, David receives official recognition as Israel's king.

> *Then all the tribes of Israel came to David at Hebron, and said, "Look, we are your bone and flesh. For some time, while Saul was king over us, it was you who led out Israel and brought it in. The LORD said to you: It is you who shall be shepherd of my people Israel, you who shall be ruler over Israel." So all the elders of Israel came to the king at Hebron; and King David made a covenant with them at Hebron before the LORD, and they anointed David king over Israel. David was thirty years old when he began to reign, and he reigned forty years. At Hebron he reigned over Judah seven years and six months; and at Jerusalem he reigned over all Israel and Judah thirty-three years. (2 Sam. 5:1–5)*

Now that he is king, David works to establish a city of God. He removes the Jebusites from Jerusalem. This will be the place for Yahweh to dwell. He also works with Hiram, king of Tyre, and employs him to build his personal house. At the same time, he acquires additional concubines, wives, and children while in Jerusalem.

> *And these are the names of those who were born to him in Jerusalem: Shammua, Shobab, Nathan, Solomon, Ibhar, Elishua, Nepheg, Japhia, Elishama, Eliada, and Eliphelet. (2 Sam. 5:15–16).*

David then moved to have the Ark of the Covenant moved to Jerusalem from the house of Abinadab. The people of Israel organized a "party train" to bring the Ark to the new city. As they made their way, a strange thing happened that caused David to become angry with Yahweh.

> *And David and all the house of Israel were celebrating before the LORD, with songs and lyres and harps and tambourines and castanets and cymbals. And when they came to the threshing floor of Nacon, Uzzah put out his hand to the ark of God and took hold of it, for the oxen stumbled. And the anger of the LORD was kindled against Uzzah, and God struck him down there because of his error, and he died there beside the ark of God. And David was angry because the LORD had broken out against Uzzah. And that place is called Perez-uzzah, to this day. (2 Sam. 6:5–8)*

Even with the unexpected, devastating death of Uzzah, David and the people continue to Jerusalem. Once they arrive, they celebrate with sacrifices, dancing, and other celebratory activities. David joins in the dancing and dances so vigorously for Yahweh—"with all his might"—he danced down to his ephod (undergarment). His wife Michal was not happy and let her feelings be known to her husband.

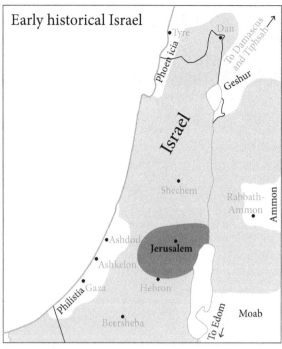

And David returned to bless his household. But Michal the daughter of Saul came out to meet David and said, "How the king of Israel honored himself today, uncovering himself today before the eyes of his servants' female servants, as one of the vulgar fellows shamelessly uncovers himself!" (2 Sam. 6:20)

Note what the writers subsequently state: "And Michal the daughter of Saul had no child to the day of her death" (2 Sam. 6:23). Also keep in mind that this is the last time the writers mention Michal.

David does establish a city of the God of Israel, builds a palace for himself, and brings the Ark of the Covenant to Jerusalem. However, he does not build a temple for Yahweh. Why? The primary reason given is based on David's previous actions:

= A rough approximate map of the lands inhabited by Israelites or under ***direct*** central royal administration during the United Monarchy (according to the Bible). This is basically what is referred to by the recurring Biblical phrase "from Dan to Beersheba".

= The central core of ancient Judea.
This area was part of a Jewish kingdom, or a Jewish province within a larger empire, almost continuously from the days of King David down to 135 CE.

FIG. 6.2 **Map of Israel during the United Monarchy**

Then King David rose to his feet and said: "Hear me, my brothers and my people. I had it in my heart to build a house of rest for the ark of the covenant of the LORD and for the footstool of our God, and I made preparations for building. But God said to me, 'You may not build a house for my name, for you are a man of war and have shed blood.'" (1 Chron. 28:2–3)

While this reason is plausible, though rooted strongly in theology, there are other possibilities or thoughts that should be considered. For instance, this is something that will come up in the following king's reign, but it may be that the people had concerns with the taxation that would come with paying for a project like this. Without question, it would have been a significant accomplishment for David to have the house of the Israelite deity constructed during his reign, but it would have incurred a tremendous expense.

David does develop a long-lasting dynasty. Yahweh even creates a covenant with him:

> When your days are fulfilled and you lie down with your fathers, I will raise up your offspring after you, who shall come from your body, and I will establish his kingdom. He shall build a house for my name, and I will establish the throne of his kingdom forever. I will be to him a father, and he shall be to me a son. When he commits iniquity, I will discipline him with the rod of men, with the stripes of the sons of men, but my steadfast love will not depart from him, as I took it from Saul, whom I put away from before you. And your house and your kingdom shall be made sure forever before me. Your throne shall be established forever."
> (2 Sam. 7:12–16)

David's personal life (Court History) is filled with entertaining adventures ranging from adultery to incest. As his kingdom continues to progress, David's life changes. It appears that he is restricted when it comes to warfare, as the writers state:

> In the spring of the year, the time when kings go out to battle, David sent Joab, and his servants with him, and all Israel. And they ravaged the Ammonites and besieged Rabbah. But David remained at Jerusalem. (2 Sam. 11:1)

Given the number of issues David has to deal with when it comes to his family, they may have affected his ability to govern his people with any real effectiveness. Along with this he has to deal with his allies and enemies. The Ammonites test him by shaving off half of David's soldiers' beards, which was the ultimate disgrace. The beard is a distinct symbol of manhood. To forcibly shave another man's beard was to destroy his manhood. Without question, David had to send troops to address this desecration.

David also had an affair that rocked his relations with those close to him (2 Sam. 11). His affair with Bathsheba, wife of Uriah the Hittite, a non-Israelite who was a dedicated solider in his army, was scandalous. Because Bathsheba became pregnant during their involvement, David attempted to cover it by having Uriah come in from the front line and sleep with his wife. However, it didn't happen. Uriah was too faithful to his fellow troops and felt he should not enjoy this pleasure while his companions were fighting. David became desperate and arranged for Uriah to be sent to the battle front lines, where the fighting was the heaviest, and he is killed. Yet the problem is not solved. A court prophet of David calls out the king's act. The baby dies. Note that David eventually marries Bathsheba, and she gives birth to a second child—a son, who will become the next king of Israel.

David's dysfunctional family problems continue, specifically with his sons Amnon and Absalom. Amnon rapes his half-sister Tamar (2 Sam. 13). Consequently, Absalom has Amnon murdered. Absalom decides to challenge to become the heir of David's throne. Absalom is exiled for this, but when he returns, he still vies for the throne. He wants to usurp the established line, and he proclaims himself king while in Hebron. Moreover, in an attempt to demonstrate authority, Absalom publicly has sex with ten of David's concubines (2 Sam. 16:20–22).

FIG. 6.3 Tell Dan inscription. This artifact may mention the house of David

David eventually has to face his son's revolt. Absalom is killed by Davidic loyalists as he hangs by his beautiful locks from a tree.

Before David goes the way of all flesh, another of his sons, Adonijah, proclaims that he will become the next king of Israel. However, a group that supports Solomon (Nathan, Bathsheba, Zadok, etc.) goes to David before he dies and makes sure that he names Solomon as the next king.

> King David answered, "Summon Bathsheba to me." So she came into the king's presence, and stood before the king. The king swore, saying, "As the LORD lives, who has saved my life from every adversity, as I swore to you by the LORD, the God of Israel, 'Your son Solomon shall succeed me as king, and he shall sit on my throne in my place,' so will I do this day." Then Bathsheba bowed with her face to the ground, and did obeisance to the king, and said, "May my lord King David live forever!" King David said, "Summon to me the priest Zadok, the prophet Nathan, and Benaiah son of Jehoiada." When they came before the king, the king said to them, "Take with you the servants of your lord, and have my son Solomon ride on my own mule, and bring him down to Gihon. There let the priest Zadok and the prophet Nathan anoint him king over Israel; then blow the trumpet, and say, 'Long live King Solomon!' You shall go up following him. Let him enter and sit on my throne; he shall be king in my place; for I have appointed him to be ruler over Israel and over Judah."

Benaiah son of Jehoiada answered the king, "Amen! May the LORD, the God of my lord the king, so ordain. As the LORD has been with my lord the king, so may he be with Solomon, and make his throne greater than the throne of my lord King David." So the priest Zadok, the prophet Nathan, and Benaiah son of Jehoiada, and the Cherethites and the Pelethites, went down and had Solomon ride on King David's mule, and led him to Gihon. There the priest Zadok took the horn of oil from the tent and anointed Solomon. Then they blew the trumpet, and all the people said, "Long live King Solomon!" And all the people went up following him, playing on pipes and rejoicing with great joy, so that the earth quaked at their noise. (1 Kings 1:28–40)

Archaeologically, there are scant artifacts and objects that make strong connections to the United Monarchy. There is a stepped stone structure in Jerusalem that may have been part of one of David's buildings. An inscription from Tel Dan may reveal aspects of David's identity. This stele is an extrabiblical text that possibly mentions the "house of David."

Solomon's Reign

As a result of the group's intervention against Adonijah, Solomon takes his place on the throne as king of the United Monarchy. The biblical writers present David and Bathsheba's son in a manner similar to the previous kings. He has specific attributes—handsome, talented, wise, and extremely intelligent. Solomon's acumen and wisdom are his most noted characteristics. How does he acquire these? In a dream, or vision, Yahweh asks him a question, and because of his response requesting wisdom, the deity blesses him immensely with this element, as well as in other areas.

Solomon loved the LORD, walking in the statutes of his father David; only, he sacrificed and offered incense at the high places. The king went to Gibeon to sacrifice there, for that was the principal high place; Solomon used to offer a thousand burnt offerings on that altar. At Gibeon the LORD appeared to Solomon in a dream by night; and God said, "Ask what I should give you." And Solomon said, "You have shown great and steadfast love to your servant my father David, because he walked before you in faithfulness, in righteousness, and in uprightness of heart toward you; and you have kept for him this great and steadfast love, and have given him a son to sit on his throne today. And now, O LORD my God, you have made your servant king in place of my father David, although I am only a little child; I do not know how to go out or come in. And your servant is in the midst of the people whom you have chosen, a great people, so numerous they cannot be numbered or counted. Give your servant therefore an understanding mind to govern your people, able to discern between good and evil; for who can govern this your great people?" It pleased the Lord that Solomon had asked this. God said to him, "Because you have asked this, and have not asked for yourself long life or riches, or for the life of your enemies, but have asked for yourself understanding to discern what is right, I now do according to your word. Indeed I give you a wise and discerning mind; no one like you has been before you and no one like you shall arise after you. I give you also what you have not asked, both riches and honor all your life; no other king shall compare with you. If you will walk in my ways, keeping my statutes and my commandments, as your father David walked, then I will lengthen your life." (1 Kings 3:3-14)

Solomon was an active administrator during his reign. He redraws the political boundaries of the tribal territories (1 Kings 4:7–19). During his time on the throne there are also lots of public construction projects that enhanced the transportation infrastructure. These actions help to further unify the country. Solomon also invests in defending Israel with construction or refurbishing of fortresses in Gezer, Hazor, and Megiddo (1 Kgs. 9:15–19). Large city gates were popular during this period; gates with six chambers were the primary entrances to large walled cities.

The new king also made a number of alliances with other countries (Egypt, Phoenicia, Sheba). Some of these are based on marriages and trade agreements. The writers state that he had 700 wives and 300 concubines. While these relationships were for the most part beneficial to the monarchy, there were many who opposed Solomon's international marriages.

Solomon also constructs the temple for Yahweh, the feat his father was not allowed to do.

Solomon began to build the house of the LORD in Jerusalem on Mount Moriah, where the LORD had appeared to his father David, at the place that David had designated, on the threshing floor of Ornan the Jebusite (2 Chron. 3:1; see also 1 Kings 5-7).

The writers also explain that the location of the temple was on Mount Moriah. The location has a possible connection with the "Binding of Isaac" (*Aqedah*, Gen. 22). In this story, God tests Abraham's faith by telling him take his son Isaac up to one of the mountains and sacrifice him. Abraham is obedient, and Isaac's life is spared. Although David did not build the temple, he had purchased the threshing floor where Solomon eventually built the structure (2 Sam. 24:18–25). Solomon dedicated the temple to Yahweh and reiterated the promise of God to David.

Then the king turned around and blessed all the assembly of Israel, while all the assembly of Israel stood. He said, "Blessed be the LORD, the God of Israel, who with his hand has fulfilled what he promised with his mouth to my father David, saying, 'Since the day that I brought my people Israel out of Egypt, I have not chosen a city from any of the tribes of Israel in which to build a house, that my name might be there; but I chose David to be over my people Israel.' My father David had it in mind to build a house for the name of the LORD, the God of Israel. But the LORD said to my father David, 'You did well to consider building a house for my name; nevertheless you shall not build the house, but your son who shall be born to you shall build the house for my name.' Now the LORD has upheld the promise that he made; for I have risen in the place of my father David; I sit on the throne of Israel, as the LORD promised, and have built the house for the name of the LORD, the God of Israel. There I have provided a place for the ark, in which is the covenant of the LORD that he made with our ancestors when he brought them out of the land of Egypt." (1 Kings 8:14–21)

An overall assessment of Solomon's reign would indicate that it was successful. However, his time on the throne comes to a somewhat tragic end. As stated, there were those who disliked Solomon's international marriages, and the writers point to this as a major factor of his downfall. The people are concerned that women from other nations will turn his attention away from Yahweh, and he will worship or entertain other deities.

King Solomon loved many foreign women along with the daughter of Pharaoh: Moabite, Ammonite, Edomite, Sidonian, and Hittite women, from the nations concerning which the LORD had said to the Israelites, "You shall not enter into marriage with them, neither shall they with you; for they will surely incline your heart to follow their gods"; Solomon clung to these in love. Among his wives were seven hundred princesses and three hundred concubines; and his wives turned away his heart. For when Solomon was old, his wives turned away his heart after other gods; and his heart was not true to the LORD his God, as was the heart of his father David. For Solomon followed Astarte the goddess of the Sidonians, and Milcom the abomination of the Ammonites. So Solomon did what was evil in the sight of the LORD, and did not completely follow the LORD, as his father

David had done. Then Solomon built a high place for Chemosh the abomination of Moab, and for Molech the abomination of the Ammonites, on the mountain east of Jerusalem. He did the same for all his foreign wives, who offered incense and sacrificed to their gods. (1 Kings 11:1–8)

It appears this is what happened. Note that although the writers state that Solomon participated in worshiping other deities besides Yahweh, he never turns away from or abandons the Israelite deity. The description they present is more of a practice of henotheism (paying homage to one main deity but still worshiping others).

In addition, heavy taxation and forced labor caused complications. The many construction projects that took place during Solomon's reign were financed by taxes and compelling people to complete the buildings. His advisers warned against this, but Solomon continued his efforts. The combination of these acts remains a part of the Solomonic legacy.

Yahweh sends the prophet Ahijah the Shilonite to Jeroboam to let him know that the kingdom will be taken from Solomon, and Jeroboam will eventually lead Israel.

The man Jeroboam was very able, and when Solomon saw that the young man was industrious he gave him charge over all the forced labor of the house of Joseph. About that time, when Jeroboam was leaving Jerusalem, the prophet Ahijah the Shilonite found him on the road. Ahijah had clothed himself with a new garment. The two of them were alone in the open country when Ahijah laid hold of the new garment he was wearing and tore it into twelve pieces. He then said to Jeroboam: Take for yourself ten pieces; for thus says the LORD, the God of Israel, "See, I am about to tear the kingdom from the hand of Solomon, and will give you ten tribes. One tribe will remain his, for the sake of my servant David and for the sake of Jerusalem, the city that I have chosen out of all the tribes of Israel. This is because he has forsaken me, worshiped Astarte the goddess of the Sidonians, Chemosh the god of Moab, and Milcom the god of the Ammonites, and has not walked in my ways, doing what is right in my sight and keeping my statutes and my ordinances, as his father David did. Nevertheless I will not take the whole kingdom away from him but will make him ruler all the days of his life, for the sake of my servant David whom I chose and who did keep my commandments and my statutes; but I will take the kingdom away from his son and give it to you—that is, the ten tribes. Yet to his son I will give one tribe, so that my servant David may always have a lamp before me in

Jerusalem, the city where I have chosen to put my name. I will take you, and you shall reign over all that your soul desires; you shall be king over Israel. If you will listen to all that I command you, walk in my ways, and do what is right in my sight by keeping my statutes and my commandments, as David my servant did, I will be with you, and will build you an enduring house, as I built for David, and I will give Israel to you. For this reason I will punish the descendants of David, but not forever." Solomon sought therefore to kill Jeroboam; but Jeroboam promptly fled to Egypt, to King Shishak of Egypt, and remained in Egypt until the death of Solomon. (1 Kings 11:28–40)

Solomon dies, and Jeroboam returns from hiding in Egypt. Jeroboam and all of Israel go to speak with Rehoboam, Solomon's son. He is now the new king of Israel. Jeroboam and Israel ask Rehoboam how he is going to rule—will it be with heavy taxes and forced labor like his father, or otherwise? Rehoboam has inherited a kingdom that has tremendous potential and success, but it could be so much more with some necessary changes. Jeroboam assures him that if he will back off the taxes and forced labor, the people will serve him mightily (1 Kings 12:4). Rehoboam responds that he will get back with them in three days. During that time, he consults with Solomon's elder advisers and then with his youthful peers. The meeting with Solomon's advisers is tense and unproductive, as they advise him to reduce taxes and labor. His friends encourage him to be more forceful than his father, but to establish himself with them. After three days, Rehoboam responds to Jeroboam and the people of Israel.

The king answered the people harshly. He disregarded the advice that the older men had given him and spoke to them according to the advice of the young men, "My father made your yoke heavy, but I will add to your yoke; my father disciplined you with whips, but I will discipline you with scorpions." So the king did not listen to the people, because it was a turn of affairs brought about by the LORD that he might fulfill his word, which the LORD had spoken by Ahijah the Shilonite to Jeroboam son of Nebat. When all Israel saw that the king would not listen to them, the people answered the king,

*"What share do we have in David?
We have no inheritance in the son of Jesse.
To your tents, O Israel!
Look now to your own house, O David."
So Israel went away to their tents. (1 Kings 12:13–16)*

FIG. 6.4 View of possible Solomonic Gate from inside Gezer, looking toward Jerusalem.

The people refuse to accept Rehoboam's new approach, and the split of the United Monarchy takes place. Jeroboam and his faction move to the northern portion of the country. Others remain in the south with Rehoboam.

Split of the Kingdom: Israel—North; Judah—South

Now that the kingdom has split, Jeroboam moves to be the king of Israel in the north, while Rehoboam remains in Judah. This abrupt change is traumatic. Israel is new and still developing, and Judah is suffering an exodus of people moving to the north. They are vulnerable. This is a problem in particular for Rehoboam and Judah. Pharaoh Shishak sees Judah's weakness and invades.

> *In the fifth year of King Rehoboam, Shishak king of Egypt came up against Jerusalem. He took away the treasures of the house of the LORD and the treasures of the king's house. He took away everything. He also took away all the shields of gold that Solomon had made, and King Rehoboam made in their place shields of bronze, and committed them to the hands of the officers of the guard, who kept the door of the king's house.*

And as often as the king went into the house of the LORD, the
guard carried them and brought them back to the guardroom.
(1 Kings 14:25–28)

Jeroboam struggles to pull matters together in Israel. Although they have split from Rehoboam and are working toward independence, there are difficulties for them in maintaining their obligations to worshiping Yahweh. Jeroboam understands that Deuteronomistic Ideology has three major components that must be maintained.

- Worship Yahweh and Yahweh only.
- Worship Yahweh according to the priests.
- Worship Yahweh only in Jerusalem.

The last one will prove to be a challenge—Jerusalem is in Judah! How can they maintain loyalty to Yahweh and adhere to this tenet of Deuteronomistic Ideology? Why should they be concerned? A closer look reveals some of the apprehensiveness:

Loyalty. If people make a major trek from the north to the south to make mandatory Yahwistic sacrifices, will they come back to the north?

Economics, Finances. Although Yahwistic sacrifices are important, all of these activities involve money in some way. Purchases for sacrifices, money spent while on the pilgrimage to and while in Judah and Jerusalem, for items such as lodging, food, and taxes These all generate revenue for the south, primarily directly from the pockets of the north. This could be detrimental financially to Jeroboam's kingdom.

Safety Concerns. How would people from the north be received in the south? Would there be skirmishes between northerners and southerners? Would people be hurt or labeled traitors?

Jeroboam seems to anticipate these major problems and decides to develop edicts that will address them. (1) He constructs cultic or religious centers at Dan (north) and Bethel (south); these areas will serve in place of the temple at Jerusalem. Here, people can fulfill the worship requirements of Deuteronomistic Ideology. The places are equipped with all necessary sacrifice items (e.g., golden calves), and they each have a *bamah* (pl. *bamot*), or high place. (2) He installed priests; they were not Levites. (3) He set specific festival days for the people of Israel.

It is important to note that all of the actions and activities still pertain to Yahweh. Jeroboam took care to make sure these were done as much as possible in accordance with Yahwistic practices and no other ideological practices. However, the south had a different view. They saw the actions as blasphemous and gave it the moniker the *Sin of Jeroboam* (1 Kings 12). Although the Sin of Jeroboam is condemned by the south, it works well for the north and lasts for centuries.

Credits

Fig. 6.1: Source: https://commons.wikimedia.org/wiki/File:MACCOUN(1899)_p081_ABOUT_1350_TO_1020_B.C._-_ISRAEL,_TIME_OF_THE_JUDGES.jpg.

Fig. 6.2: Source: https://commons.wikimedia.org/wiki/File:Early-Historical-Israel-Dan-Beersheba-Judea.png.

Fig. 6.3: Copyright © Oren Rozen (CC BY-SA 4.0) at https://en.wikipedia.org/wiki/Tel_Dan_Stele#/media/File:JRSLM_300116_Tel_Dan_Stele_01.jpg.

Fig. 6.4: Copyright © Ian Scott (CC BY-SA 2.0) at https://commons.wikimedia.org/wiki/File:Six-chambered_gate_at_Tel_Gezer_(5751793235).jpg.

CHAPTER 7

Prophets in Ancient Israel

WHAT IS A prophet? The term comes from the Hebrew root *nebi* or *nevi*, "to announce, call, or speak." The title prophet, or referring to someone as a prophet, is a fairly common occurrence. Think about someone today whom you would call a prophet. Why? What does this mean? What is meant when one is labeled as a prophet? What characteristics does that person exemplify to be a bearer of that label? The following discussion gives a brief overview of prophets in the Hebrew Bible/Old Testament. It shares information about several individuals closely linked to the culture in ancient Israel.

Some Characteristics of a Prophet

How did a person become a prophet in antiquity? It is not always clear how this happens. Some figures appear out of nowhere (e.g., Elijah), already branded as prophets; in other instances, the writers provide a detailed backstory (e.g., Amos). There are also prophets who have a *call narrative*. Call narratives explain how the prophet is "called" by the deity to be a spokesperson and share specific messages. For example, there are call narratives for the prophets Samuel, Isaiah, and Jeremiah.

Samuel:

> Now the boy Samuel was ministering to the LORD in the presence of Eli. And the word of the LORD was rare in those days; there was no frequent vision. At that time Eli, whose eyesight had begun to grow dim so that he could not see, was lying down in his own place. The lamp of God had not yet gone out, and Samuel was lying down in the temple of the LORD, where the ark of God was. Then the LORD called Samuel, and he said, "Here I am!" and ran to Eli and said, "Here I am, for you called me." But he said, "I did not call; lie down again." So he went and lay down. And the LORD called again, "Samuel!" and Samuel arose and went to Eli and said, "Here I am, for you called me." But he said, "I did not call, my son; lie down again."

> *Now Samuel did not yet know the LORD, and the word of the LORD had not yet been revealed to him. And the LORD called Samuel again the third time. And he arose and went to Eli and said, "Here I am, for you called me." Then Eli perceived that the LORD was calling the boy. Therefore Eli said to Samuel, "Go, lie down, and if he calls you, you shall say, 'Speak, LORD, for your servant hears.'" So Samuel went and lay down in his place. (1 Sam. 3:1–9)*

Isaiah:

> *And I heard the voice of the LORD saying, "Whom shall I send, and who will go for us?" Then I said, "Here I am! Send me." And he said, "Go, and say to this people:*
>
> *'Keep on hearing, but do not understand;*
> *keep on seeing, but do not perceive.'" (Isa. 6:8–9)*

Jeremiah:

> *Now the word of the LORD came to me, saying,*
>
> *"Before I formed you in the womb I knew you, and before you were born I consecrated you; I appointed you a prophet to the nations." (Jer. 1:4–5)*

While prophets are often called by the deity, it doesn't always mean they want to answer. Consider Jonah, who resisted Yahweh vehemently:

> *Now the word of the LORD came to Jonah son of Amittai, saying, "Go at once to Nineveh, that great city, and cry out against it; for their wickedness has come up before me." But Jonah set out to flee to Tarshish from the presence of the LORD. He went down to Joppa and found a ship going to Tarshish; so he paid his fare and went on board, to go with them to Tarshish, away from the presence of the LORD. (Jon. 1:1–3)*

Nevertheless, the prophets eventually answered the divine call.

Although the biblical text doesn't always give background information or the place of origin for each prophet, each appears to be special or unique in some way. Most prophets share the following characteristics:

- spokesperson for the deity or for those who can't effectively speak for themselves
- connected with a deity or deities
- critics of wrongdoing in society
- charismatic

"Thus says…"

It is important to note that prophets had to be very careful about the words they spoke connected to prophecy. When uttering prophecies from a deity, they were not speaking personally. Prophets were representatives; when delivering prophecies, they never speak in their own name. When providing messages in the name of the deity, the words possess heavy authority. The biblical prophetic books and their passages often employ the prophetic formula, "Thus says Yahweh" ("Thus says the LORD"). Remember, when it comes to prophets, it's all about the message.

The prophets' delivery can be fascinating and entertaining. Drama and theatrics were common. Jeremiah is described wearing a prop:

> *In the beginning of the reign of King Zedekiah son of Josiah of Judah, this word came to Jeremiah from the LORD. Thus the LORD said to me: Make yourself a yoke of straps and bars, and put them on your neck. (Jer. 27:1–2)*

Isaiah walked naked and barefoot:

> *Then the LORD said, "Just as my servant Isaiah has walked naked and barefoot for three years as a sign and a portent against Egypt and Ethiopia, so shall the king of Assyria lead away the Egyptians as captives and the Ethiopians as exiles, both the young and the old, naked and barefoot, with buttocks uncovered, to the shame of Egypt. (Isa. 20:3–4)*

Ezekiel lay on his side:

> *And you, O mortal, take a brick and set it before you. On it portray a city, Jerusalem; and put siegeworks against it, and build a siege wall against it, and cast up a ramp against it; set camps also against it, and plant battering rams against it all around. Then take an iron plate and place it as an iron wall*

between you and the city; set your face toward it, and let it be in a state of siege, and press the siege against it. This is a sign for the house of Israel. Then lie on your left side, and place the punishment of the house of Israel upon it; you shall bear their punishment for the number of the days that you lie there. For I assign to you a number of days, three hundred ninety days, equal to the number of the years of their punishment; and so you shall bear the punishment of the house of Israel. When you have completed these, you shall lie down a second time, but on your right side, and bear the punishment of the house of Judah; forty days I assign you, one day for each year. You shall set your face toward the siege of Jerusalem, and with your arm bared you shall prophesy against it. See, I am putting cords on you so that you cannot turn from one side to the other until you have completed the days of your siege. (Ezek. 4:1–8)

These types of theatrics would attract an audience to hear their messages.

Prophetic Vocabulary

Prophets had to know their audiences and how to communicate information effectively to them. Their choice of words had to be effective and relatable. It would be pointless for them to use "highfalutin'" terms or speak about analogies and similes outside of their daily lives. Thus, prophets often used agrarian language, everyday metaphors, familiar symbols, or references to aspects of the culture. Those that would have heard prophets using this kind of verbiage could better comprehend and relate to the messages.

Types of Prophets

Prophets were ubiquitous, but not all of their names and words were recorded. Keep in mind that all of the writings we read would have been written down after the discussed events. Most would have come from oral traditions. For the most part, prophets in Israel fall into one of three types.

Court Prophets. These were prophets that worked specifically for the king. Nathan was a prophet in King David's court (2 Sam. 12).

Cult Community Prophets. These were prophets that lived among the people; they were a part of the community (e.g., Isaiah).

Peripheral Prophets. These were prophets who were independent of any king or political power. They survived on the most part on their own, with some help from the prophetic community or "sons of the prophets" (e.g., Elijah, Elisha).

Things Not to Do to Communicate with Yahweh

There were a number of ways prophets attempted to glean prophetic information from Yahweh. For instance, Elisha used music:

> Elisha said, "As the LORD of hosts lives, whom I serve, were it not that I have regard for King Jehoshaphat of Judah, I would give you neither a look nor a glance. But get me a musician." And then, while the musician was playing, the power of the LORD came on him. (2 Kings 3:14–15)

> However, there were certain ways of attempting to commune with Yahweh that were prohibited to them:

- No divination (the practice of seeking knowledge of the future or the unknown by supernatural means)
- No passing children through the fire; those that worshipped the god Molech often passed children through fire to learn a prophecy
- No soothsaying (soothsayer: a person supposed to be able to force the future)
- No sorcery (the use of magic);
- no casting spells (a form of words used as a magical charm or incantation)
- No necromancy (the practice of communicating with the dead);
- no consulting ghosts;
- no consulting mediums to contact ghosts

Getting or Receiving the Prophetic Message

According to the biblical writers, Yahweh often gave or put the message in the prophet's mouth. In other words, the deity told the individual what to say, and in some instances, how to say it. Also, the deity communicated with individuals through dreams and vision. Some employed the casting or throwing of lots, such as Urim and Thummim.

> In the breastpiece of judgment you shall put the Urim and the Thummim, and they shall be on Aaron's heart when he goes in before the LORD; thus Aaron shall bear the judgment of the Israelites on his heart before the LORD continually. (Exod. 28:30)

> "O LORD God of Israel, why have you not answered your servant today? If this guilt is in me or in my son Jonathan, O LORD God of Israel, give Urim; but if this guilt is in your people Israel,

give Thummim." And Jonathan and Saul were indicated by the lot, but the people were cleared. Then Saul said, "Cast the lot between me and my son Jonathan." And Jonathan was taken. (1 Sam.14:41–42)

These looked for their entries in the genealogical records, but they were not found there, and so they were excluded from the priesthood as unclean; the governor told them that they were not to partake of the most holy food, until there should be a priest to consult Urim and Thummim. (Ezra 2:62–63)

Prophets and prophecy were known throughout the ancient Near East. Their practices varied, but for the most part, prophets desired to obtain and disseminate messages from the deity. Some ways of doing this that were known throughout the area include the following:

- Augury: the study of the flight patterns of birds
- Astrology: the study of the movements and relative positions of celestial bodies interpreted as having an influence on human affairs and the natural world
- Extispicy: divination by means of inspecting the entrails of sacrificed animals, especially sheep and goats
- Kleromancy/Cleromancy: casting or throwing of lots (e.g., dice, beans, seeds)
- Astragali: casting or throwing of animal knuckle bones
- Arrows: dropping of arrows and reading how they fall
- Pur: casting or throwing of dice
- Oneiromancy: interpretation of dreams

Prophets of the Hebrew Bible/Old Testament

Although prophets and prophecies are not discussed in detail in this book, one should be aware of the prophetic books of the Hebrew Bible/Old Testament.

Isaiah: divided into three parts with specific dates; the first, chapters 1–39, date to 701 BCE; the second, Deutero-Isaiah, chapters 40–66, sixth century BCE, and Trito-Isaiah, chapters 56–66, possibly late sixth century BCE (ca. 500)

Jeremiah: dates to seventh–sixth centuries BCE; Yahwistic prophet

Lamentations: five poems lamenting destruction of temple

Ezekiel: dates to the 6th century BCE; prophet is noted for discussion the judgement and blessing of Israel and other nations; six visions

Daniel: dates possibly dating to sixth century BCE; he was taken into Babylonian captivity; discusses life in Babylonian captivity

Hosea: dates to the eighth century BCE; Israelite marries unfaithful woman, which is a possible metaphor for the relationship between God and Israel

Joel: dates span ninth–sixth centuries BCE; prophet speaks of young men seeing visions, sons and daughters prophesying;

Amos: dates to the 8th century BCE; prophet discusses economic issues and problems between the rich and poor

Obadiah: dates to the sixth century BCE; discusses the fall of Edom, Babylonian captivity

Jonah: dates to the 8th century BCE; possibly written during the post exilic period; prophet assigned to speak to the Assyrians

Micah: dates to the 8th century BCE; speaks about the problems of Jerusalem and Samaria; prophet was a contemporary of Isaiah

Nahum: dates possibly to the seventh century BCE; discusses the fall of Nineveh, capital of Assyria

Habakkuk: dates to seventh century BCE; little is known about the prophet; the book contains song, elements of psalms of lament

Zephaniah: dates to the seventh century BCE; prophet said to be the great-great grandson of King Hezekiah; speaks against idolatry

Nahum: possibly dating to the 7th century BCE, the end of Josiah's reign; short book; not much known about the prophet

Haggai: dates to sixth century BCE; prophet encourages people to build the second temple in Jerusalem

Zechariah: dates to the sixth century BCE; prophesies about the return to Jerusalem and Israel's salvation

Malachi: dates possibly to sixth century BCE or later; discusses taxes, tithes, and how this should work

Elijah and Elisha Cycle Narratives

Two prophets stand out during the Divided Monarchy—Elijah and Elisha. Elijah appeared on the scene during the Omride Dynasty, specifically during the reign of Ahab and Jezebel. He doesn't have a specific call narrative, but we learn that he is a Tishbite, from Tishbe (1 Kings 17:1). Jezebel was from Phoenicia and brought Baalism to the Israelites when she and Ahab married. Elijah is a Yahwistic prophet and has encounters with Ahab, Jezebel, Baalism, and those not following Yahweh only (e.g., the battle on Mt. Carmel, 1 Kings 18:30–40). He survives an array of situations but remains faithful to Yahweh.

Elisha connects with Elijah and begins his process to become his successor. He, however, has a brief call narrative (1 Kings 19:19–21). Once he accepts his call, there is a magnificent event in which Elijah places his mantle on Elisha's shoulders, signifying the transfer of authority, before Elijah is taken up into the heavens by a chariot. Elisha continues the prophetic work and promotes Yahwism over all else. He also demonstrates one of the many ways to obtain a prophecy when he requires a musician (2 Kings 3:13–20). In contrast to his predecessor, Elisha dies (2 Kings 13:14–20), and his bones, much like the mantle of Elijah, hold power (2 Kings 13:20–21).

CHAPTER 8

Late Monarchic Period

Fall of Israel and Judah

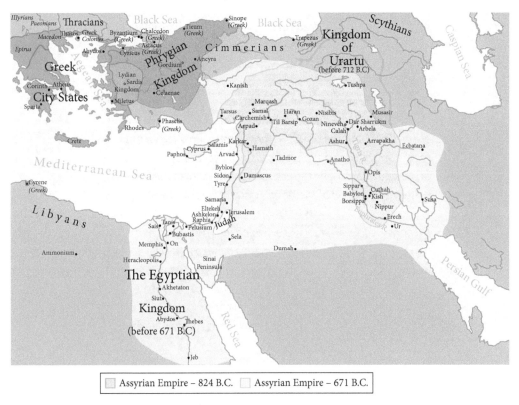

FIG. 8.1 **Map of the Assyrian Empire**

Fall of Israel

In the midst of the battle for supremacy in the Near East and parts of Africa, Assyria begins to emerge again. Since the tenth–ninth century BCE, the Assyrians have been getting stronger, starting what is known as the Neo-Assyrian period (911–627 BCE). Egypt is still a challenger, but Assyria is developing its legendary military prowess and increasing in dominance. Several kings lead the country in a massive westward campaign.

Life in Israel is chaotic. Because the monarchy is divided, there is constant instability. Between 900 and 750 BCE, this is the case in particular in the north. Israel's kingship is suffering from usurpation, assassinations, and military takeovers. Thus, there is little reliability or regularity in the leadership. An attempted coup by a power hungry Zimri sheds light on Israel's situation. Zimri's coup helped to usher in the Omride Dynasty.

In the twenty-seventh year of King Asa of Judah, Zimri reigned seven days in Tirzah. Now the troops were encamped against Gibbethon, which belonged to the Philistines, and the troops who were encamped heard it said, "Zimri has conspired, and he has killed the king"; therefore all Israel made Omri, the commander of the army, king over Israel that day in the camp. So Omri went up from Gibbethon, and all Israel with him, and they besieged Tirzah. When Zimri saw that the city was taken, he went into the citadel of the king's house; he burned down the king's house over himself with fire, and died—because of the sins that he committed, doing evil in the sight of the LORD, walking in the way of Jeroboam, and for the sin that he committed, causing Israel to sin. Now the rest of the acts of Zimri, and the conspiracy that he made, are they not written in the Book of the Annals of the Kings of Israel?

Then the people of Israel were divided into two parts; half of the people followed Tibni son of Ginath, to make him king, and half followed Omri. But the people who followed Omri overcame the people who followed Tibni son of Ginath; so Tibni died, and Omri became king. In the thirty-first year of King Asa of Judah, Omri began to reign over Israel; he reigned for twelve years, six of them in Tirzah.

He bought the hill of Samaria from Shemer for two talents of silver; he fortified the hill, and called the city that he built, Samaria, after the name of Shemer, the owner of the hill. Omri did what was evil in the sight of the LORD; he did more evil than all who were before him. For he walked in all the way of Jeroboam son of Nebat, and in the sins that he caused Israel to commit, provoking the LORD, the God of Israel, to anger by their idols. Now the rest of the acts of Omri that he did, and the power that he showed, are they not written in the Book of the Annals of the Kings of Israel? Omri slept with his ancestors, and was buried in Samaria; his son Ahab succeeded him. (1 Kings 16:15–28)

Elijah and Elisha had battles with King Ahab, son of Omri, and his wife, Jezebel. As mentioned previously, Jezebel was from the coast of Phoenicia, and she introduced Baalism to Israel. Eventually, Baalism and the worship of Yahweh came into competition (1 Kings 18:17–18). Elijah and Elisha were determined to do all they could to thwart Jezebel's attempt to have Baalism take over and eradicate Yahweh. Nevertheless, while Baalism did not overtake Yahweh, it became a major part of the culture. For example, Judahite king, Manasseh, son of Hezekiah, reigned 55 years practicing polytheism (2 Kings 21:1–6). The pantheon at that time included Yahweh, Baal, Asherah, and others. Although there was immense turmoil in Israel politically and religiously, a king emerged who was a strong follower of Yahweh. That figure was Jehu. Jehu accepted an invitation from Elisha, the prophetic successor to Elijah, to overthrow the Omride Dynasty. Jehu was a zealous monotheist. When Jehu revolted, he was determined to remove anyone and anything that was not dedicated to Yahweh.

Now Ahab had seventy sons in Samaria. So Jehu wrote letters and sent them to Samaria, to the rulers of Jezreel, to the elders, and to the guardians of the sons of Ahab, saying, "Since your master's sons are with you and you have at your disposal chariots and horses, a fortified city, and weapons, select the son of your master who is the best qualified, set him on his father's throne, and fight for your master's house." But they were utterly terrified and said, "Look, two kings could not withstand him; how then can we stand?" So the steward of the palace, and the governor of the city, along with the elders and the guardians, sent word to Jehu: "We are your servants; we will do anything you say. We will not make anyone king; do whatever you think right." Then he wrote them a second letter, saying, "If you are on my side, and if you are ready to obey me, take the heads of your master's sons and come to me at Jezreel tomorrow at this time." Now the king's sons, seventy persons, were with the leaders of the city, who were charged with their upbringing. When the letter reached them, they took the king's sons and killed them, seventy persons; they put their heads in baskets and sent them to him at Jezreel. When the messenger came and told him, "They have brought the heads of the king's sons," he said, "Lay them in two heaps at the entrance of the gate until the morning." Then in the morning when he went out, he stood and said to all the people, "You are innocent. It was I who conspired against my master and killed him; but who struck down all these? Know then that there shall fall to the earth nothing of the word of the LORD, which the LORD spoke concerning the house of Ahab; for the LORD has done what he said through his servant Elijah." So Jehu killed all

who were left of the house of Ahab in Jezreel, all his leaders, close
friends, and priests, until he left him no survivor. (2 Kings 10:1–11).

Jehu's zealousness was admirable, but it was also to his detriment. In his attempt to turn hearts to Yahweh only, Jehu killed everyone that opposed him or was connected to anything other than Yahweh. However, Jehu was not an administrator and did not understand the requirements to run a kingdom. In his revolt, Jehu massacred all who could have possibly helped Israel sustain itself. As a result, the burgeoning Assyrian juggernaut forced Israel into a precarious predicament. In order to maintain a semblance of independence, a tribute must be paid to Assyria. Jehu brought monotheism to the forefront, but his lack of administrative leadership turned Israel into a vassal of Assyria. An obelisk displays Jehu bowing before the Assyrian King Shalmaneser to pay the demanded funds.

Of the numerous Assyrian kings in the country's lineage during the Neo-Assyrian Period, there are three that are important to understanding the demise of Israel.

TABLE 8.1

Neo-Assyrian Kings	Period of Reign
Shalmaneser III	859–824 BCE
Tiglath-Pileser III (TP-III)	745–727 BCE
Shalmaneser V	727–722 BCE

FIG. 8.2 Scene from Assyrian Black Obelisk showing Jehu bowing before the Assyrian King Shalmaneser III

A Brief Exploration of the Hebrew Bible/Old Testament

Shalmaneser III

Shalmaneser III is an initiator of the Assyrian westward crusade. One of the most memorable moments of Shalmaneser's campaigns was the Battle of Qarqur (also spelled Karkar; located in Syria) in 835 BCE. Here, the Assyrian king battled against allied forces that had banded together to destroy him. He battled this group again later in Israel. Neither of the wars were won decisively on either side, but Shalmaneser had nevertheless success in his westward maneuvers once the coalition disintegrated. His progress set the stage for the coming Assyrian kings to gain control of the region.

Tiglath-Pileser III

Tiglath-Pileser III usurped the Assyrian throne in 745 BCE. This king is often credited with taking the Assyrian westward campaign to the next level. He has big plans. He's thinking expansion for the country, far-reaching power, a surfeit of riches, and wide-spread control. TP-III is well aware of what the territories beyond the Euphrates have to offer in the way of natural resources (lumber, metals, water sources, etc.). Possibly even more important, the lands west of Assyria were also the gateway to commerce with Egypt, Asia Minor, and the entire Mediterranean. He saw all of this as ripe for the taking because there was no group to pose any real challenge, and he decided to do so. Egypt would have been the biggest threat at this time, but they weren't in a position to do anything substantial. As TP-III led his powerful forces through the ancient Near East, he employed the interestingly brilliant tactic of deportation of groups they conquered. In this form of deportation, the Assyrians would subdue a people and gather all who had specific, useful skills (e.g., carpenters, architects, etc.), take them to a designated space, and have them build a city to desired Assyrian specifics. Once the construction was complete, the Assyrians transported in their own citizens and moved the deportees to another location to have them construct another city for more Assyrians.

Shalmaneser V

Shalmaneser V is credited with the actual fall of Israel in 722 BCE. Although his reign is brief, Shalmaneser V brings the culmination of a series of events that contribute to Israel's demise.

Briefly, in 734 BCE, Ahaz, then king of Judah, got caught in a squeeze play. Pekah, king of Israel, Rezin king of Aram (Syria), the Edomites, the Philistines, and others attempted to force Ahaz to go with them against T-P III and the invading Assyrians. This contingent often bears the title the *Damascus Coalition*. Ahaz has some concerns about this. However, instead of protesting in silence, Ahaz squeals to the Assyrians about the developing coalition and their plans. T-P III comes to investigate. As a result, he obliterates the group, sacks Damascus, and executes Rezin, King of Aram (2 Kings 16).

After reigning 20 years in Israel, King Pekah is assassinated. This is ironic, as he had murdered the previous king, Pekahiah, to gain the throne. Ahaz is still king of Judah at this time. Both Israel and Judah are subjects of Assyria, paying the requested tribute in order to keep some sense of sovereignty. After a series of events, King Pekah is assassinated by Hoshea. Once Hoshea takes the throne, the Assyrian king, TP-III, dies (727 BCE). Hoshea sees this as a chance to change Israel's situation. He attempts to talk Egypt into joining him to go against Assyria in what appears to be a moment of weakness. Egypt declines. Hoshea also decides to revolt against the new king, Shalmaneser V, and stops paying tribute. Shalmaneser easily and quickly sweeps Israel's army aside. In three years, Assyria destroys Samaria (capital of Israel) and pulls what remains into their growing provincial system. In 722 BCE, Shalmaneser destroys the remainder of the country, and what we have known as Israel is no more. Some attribute the demise of Israel to Sargon I because his reign overlaps with the brief reign of Shalmaneser V. However, most give credit to Shalmaneser V. In the same manner as TP-III, the Assyrians deported the remaining Israelites. Some were also taken back to Assyria.

It should be understood that the Assyrians were superb military strategists, as well as masters of intimidation. Assyrians often attempted to give groups they were about to conquer opportunities to surrender. At times, they employed the services of an individual called the Rabshekeh ("chief of the princes"). This person often attended to the needs of kings, but he also worked to intimidate groups to turn over their land and goods without force. To do this, the Rabshekeh would stand near the gate or wall of a city and speak disparagingly about the people in an effort to have them surrender. For example:

> *Then Eliakim the son of Hilkiah, and Shebnah, and Joah, said to the Rabshakeh, "Please speak to your servants in Aramaic, for we understand it. Do not speak to us in the language of Judah within the hearing of the people who are on the wall." But the Rabshakeh said to them, "Has my master sent me to speak these words to your master and to you, and not to the men sitting on the wall, who are doomed with you to eat their own dung and to drink their own urine?" (2 Kings 18:26–27)*

The Assyrians also strategically employed terroristic tactics such as dismemberment, impaling, and other forms of psychological warfare.

STUDY QUESTIONS

1. Can you explain why Israel fell?
2. What were historical reasons for the fall?
3. What were religious reasons for the fall?

Fall of Judah

We enter the fall of Judah beginning with the reign of Josiah in 622 BCE. How do the biblical writers describe Josiah?

> *Josiah was eight years old when he began to reign; he reigned thirty-one years in Jerusalem. His mother's name was Jedidah daughter of Adaiah of Bozkath. He did what was right in the sight of the LORD, and walked in all the way of his father David; he did not turn aside to the right or to the left. (2 Kings 22:1–2)*

The writers like this young man. He comes to the throne at eight years old (his father was assassinated) and reigns 31 years. He does what is right, or good in the eyes of Yahweh. They even compare Josiah to the most prominent and well-liked king of Israel, David. It's clear that Josiah, son of Amon, is a good guy, but what is so special about him? His claim to fame is his reformation.

When Josiah comes into power, Judah was practicing forms of henotheism and polytheism. But something happens in the 18th year of Josiah's reign, while renovations are being done in the temple. The high priest Hilkiah has "found" the book of the Law. He and Shaphan, Hilkiah's secretary, take the scroll to Josiah. When Josiah hears the words of the scroll, he tears his clothes. He realizes they have not been following Yahweh properly. Josiah acts immediately. He sends Hilkiah, Shaphan, and others to the prophetess Huldah to find out what Yahweh has to say and what they should do.

> *So the priest Hilkiah, Ahikam, Achbor, Shaphan, and Asaiah went to the prophetess Huldah the wife of Shallum son of Tikvah, son of Harhas, keeper of the wardrobe; she resided in Jerusalem in the Second Quarter, where they consulted her. She declared to them, "Thus says the LORD, the God of Israel: Tell the man who sent you to me, Thus says the LORD, I will indeed bring disaster on this place and on its inhabitants—all the words of the book that the king of Judah has read. Because they have abandoned me and have made offerings to other gods, so that they have provoked me to anger with all the work of their hands, therefore my wrath will be kindled against this place, and it will not be quenched. But as to the king of Judah, who sent you to inquire of the LORD, thus shall you say to him, Thus says the LORD, the God of Israel: Regarding the words that you have heard, because your heart was penitent, and you humbled yourself before the LORD, when you heard how I spoke against this place,*

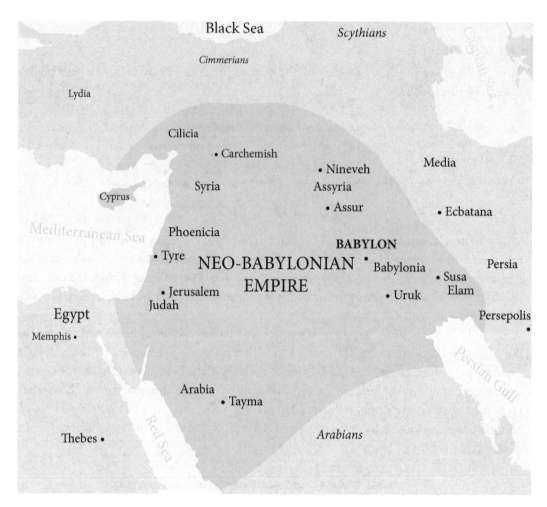

FIG. 8.3 Map of the Babylonian Empire

and against its inhabitants, that they should become a desolation and a curse, and because you have torn your clothes and wept before me, I also have heard you, says the LORD. Therefore, I will gather you to your ancestors, and you shall be gathered to your grave in peace; your eyes shall not see all the disaster that I will bring on this place." They took the message back to the king. (2 Kings 22:14–20)

Once Josiah learns what Huldah conveys from Yahweh, he goes into action.

Josiah goes to the temple and summons all the inhabitants of Jerusalem. He then reads the book to the people, they make a covenant before Yahweh to reform, to begin worshipping and honoring Yahweh properly. These activities include:

- Remove from the temple vessels for Baal, Asherah, and the host of heaven
- Depose all of the idolatrous priests whom the previous kings of Judah had ordained to make offerings at high places in cities of Judah and around Jerusalem
- Destroy images of Asherah
- Depose temple prostitutes
- Reinstitute Passover
- Pull down altars at Dan and Bethel (Sin of Jeroboam)

Josiah's powerful reformation was instituted throughout Judah. There was no one like Josiah. He served with all his heart, soul, and might. He centralized Jerusalem, which was the goal of Deuteronomistic Ideology:

- Worship Yahweh and Yahweh only.
- Worship Yahweh according to the priests.
- Worship Yahweh only in Jerusalem.

Josiah went the way of all flesh. As happens with great empires, Assyria was weakening. Babylon was on the rise. In 612 BCE, Nineveh, the capital city of Assyria, had fallen to Babylon. Also during this time, Assyria was forming an alliance with Egypt. However, in 609 BCE, before the alliance came together, Josiah went up to Megiddo to assist the last remnant of the Assyrian Empire against Pharaoh Neco, king of Egypt. Although Josiah was in revolt against Assyria, he attempted to help them and was killed by Neco. Judah became a vassal of Egypt. Assyria had to focus on the fast-approaching Babylonians.

The following section is a summary of the major events that lead to the fall of Judah. Again, because this textbook is an introduction, one of the goals is to help make the information as understandable as possible without losing meaning or omitting important intricacies.

Fall of Judah

609–605 BCE: Judah was under Egyptian domination.

605 BCE: Nebuchadnezzar of Babylon launched a surprise attack on the Egyptians at Carchemish and defeated them. The Babylonians were now in control of Syria. Jehoiakim then transferred his allegiance from Egypt to the new power in the land—Babylon. Judah paid tribute to them.

601 BCE: Nebuchadnezzar once again battled Egypt—and it was pretty close to being a draw— some could argue that the Egyptians won. In any case, Jehoiakim saw this as a moment of weakness and attempted to rebel against Babylon. Big mistake! Nebuchadnezzar responded by sending troops to Judah.

598 BCE: The full Babylonian army arrived in Jerusalem. Jehoiakim died the same month of their arrival. This was more than likely an assassination.

597 BCE: Jehoiachin was 18 years old when he was placed on the throne.

The Babylonians also employed deportation. There are three deportations that bring to Judah to an end.

First Deportation. 597 BCE. The elites were taken. Who would the elite people of a society be? Remember, these would be skilled individuals such as artisans, carpenters, and engineers. The elites were taken and spread everywhere; however, the best of the best were taken back to Babylon. This way, the Babylonians could monitor them. Also, Zedekiah, Jehoiachin's uncle, the last king of Judah, was placed on the throne by Nebuchadnezzar. He was a mere puppet king; Babylon was the real power. Nevertheless, Zedekiah decided to rebel, although Jeremiah warned him not to do this (Jer. 37–38).

> *Zedekiah son of Josiah, whom King Nebuchadnezzar of Babylon made king in the land of Judah, succeeded Coniah son of Jehoiakim. But neither he nor his servants nor the people of the land listened to the words of the LORD that he spoke through the prophet Jeremiah. (Jer. 37:1–2)*

Second Deportation. 587–586 BCE. Jerusalem was destroyed. Only the poorest of people remained in the land. The walls of Jerusalem were torn down. The Yahwistic cult was destroyed, and Deuteronomistic Yahwism was gone, at least for the time being. Gediliah, son of Solomon, was made governor in Mizpah, which is about 15 miles from Jerusalem, by Nebuchadnezzar. Gediliah was a member of a prominent Jerusalem family; his father and grandfather served in Josiah's court. The Babylonians purposely moved the remaining people away from the religious center, and it put a Babylonian stamp on the destruction of Jerusalem.

Third Deportation. 582 BCE. Gediliah had some success in governing the remaining people with the support of former officers, but he was assassinated. The governor was well respected and well liked, even by those in Babylonian captivity. There was a national day of fasting and mourning to mark his murder. The remaining people revolted—again, but the uprising was quickly squashed. Those that survived were taken and deported. Thus ended what we have known as Judah.

The 70 years of Babylonian Exile (587–539 BCE) comes to end with the invasion of the Persians, led by Cyrus the Persian. Cyrus is seen as hero by those in Babylon because he liberates them. He tells them to go home and rebuild, which initiates the beginning of the Second Temple Period. The writers Ezra, Nehemiah, and others share tales of what happened during this process.

Credits

Fig. 8.1: Source: https://commons.wikimedia.org/wiki/File:Map_of_Assyria.png.

Fig. 8.2: Copyright © Steven G. Johnson (CC BY-SA 3.0) at https://commons.wikimedia.org/wiki/File:Jehu-Obelisk-cropped.jpg.

Fig. 8.3: Source: https://commons.wikimedia.org/wiki/File:Neo-Babylonian_Empire.png.

CHAPTER 9

Wisdom Literature

W HAT IS WISDOM? How does one acquire wisdom? Where do we obtain wisdom? Wisdom is an essential theme of the Hebrew Bible/Old Testament. Its importance is demonstrated, as the text contains a section labeled Wisdom Literature. It includes the following books: Job, Psalms, Proverbs, Ecclesiastes, Song of Songs/Song of Solomon. The passages, stories and many of its characters are designed to teach and share thoughts about wisdom, morality, and approaches to living. For example: Jethro, Moses's father-in-law, gives him sage advice regarding how to govern and administer when it comes to people.

> *"Now listen to me. I will give you counsel, and God be with you! You should represent the people before God, and you should bring their cases before God; teach them the statutes and instructions and make known to them the way they are to go and the things they are to do. You should also look for able men among all the people, men who fear God, are trustworthy, and hate dishonest gain; set such men over them as officers over thousands, hundreds, fifties and tens. Let them sit as judges for the people at all times; let them bring every important case to you, but decide every minor case themselves. So it will be easier for you, and they will bear the burden with you. If you do this, and God so commands you, then you will be able to endure, and all these people will go to their home in peace." (Exod. 18:19–23)*

Solomon creatively administers justice between two women regarding a child.

> *The king said, "Divide the living boy in two; then give half to the one, and half to the other." But the woman whose son was alive said to the king—because compassion for her son burned within her—"Please, my lord, give her the living boy; certainly do not kill him!" The other said, "It shall be neither mine nor yours; divide it." Then the king responded: "Give the first woman the living boy; do not kill him. She is his mother." All Israel heard of the*

*judgment that the king had rendered; and they stood in awe of
the king, because they perceived that the wisdom of God was
in him, to execute justice. (1 Kings 3:25–28)*

Note that a section of the Hebrew Bible/Old Testament has been titled "Wisdom Literature," which demonstrates its importance. Following are the books that make up the Wisdom Literature portion of the texts.

Book of Proverbs. Proverbs, or wise sayings, are found in cultures throughout the ancient Near East. This book of the Hebrew Bible/Old Testament contains a collection of wise sayings, which come from all walks of life in Israelite culture. While they can be interesting to read, it appears that some precise meanings have been lost over time, especially when the text has not been used or presented in context. Check out this proverbs from the biblical text:

*Do not eat the bread of the stingy; do not desire their delicacies;
for like a hair in the throat, so are they. "Eat and drink!" they say
to you; but they do not mean it. (Prov. 23:6–7)*

*Do not speak in the hearing of a fool, who will only despise the
wisdom of your words. (Prov. 23:9)*

Book of Ecclesiastes. This book is often attributed to Solomon, typically because of the first verse. The primary theme is that "all is vanity"—everything will pass away eventually. The most well-known portion begins in chapter 3, where the writer explains that there is a time for almost everything.

For everything there is a season, and a time for every matter under heaven:

*a time to be born, and a time to die;
a time to plant, and a time to pluck up what is planted;
a time to kill, and a time to heal;
a time to break down, and a time to build up;
a time to weep, and a time to laugh;
a time to mourn, and a time to dance. (Eccles. 3:1–4)*

Book of Job. This book contains an intriguing story that presents a discussion between Yahweh and Ha-Satan (The Adversary) and the testing of a man named Job, who lives in the land of Luz. After a talk between Yahweh and Ha-Satan, Job becomes the center of a lengthy, very trying test. Yet Job remains steadfast in his dedication and love for Yahweh.

> *Then Job arose, tore his robe, shaved his head, and fell on the ground and worshiped. He said, "Naked I came from my mother's womb, and naked shall I return there; the LORD gave, and the LORD has taken away; blessed be the name of the LORD." (Job 1:20–21)*

Book of Psalms. This book contains a collection of 150 psalms (songs) that are on the subject of laments, hymns, or other topics. David receives credit for being the composer of the psalms; however, it should be understood that there were many who contributed to the psalter. The headings found at the beginning of a number of psalms are *superscriptions.* They often share information regarding instrumentation, choir guilds, or how they may have been sung.

Communal Lament:

> *To the leader. Of the Korahites. A Maskil.*
> *1 We have heard with our ears, O God,*
> *our ancestors have told us,*
> *what deeds you performed in their days,*
> *in the days of old:*
> *2 you with your own hand drove out the nations,*
> *but them you planted;*
> *you afflicted the peoples,*
> *but them you set free. (Ps. 44:0–2)*

Royal Psalm:

> *To the leader. A Psalm of David the servant of the LORD, who addressed the words of this song to the LORD on the day when the LORD delivered him from the hand of all his enemies, and from the hand of Saul. He said:*
>
> *1 I love you, O LORD, my strength.*
> *2 The LORD is my rock, my fortress, and my deliverer,*
> *my God, my rock in whom I take refuge,*
> *my shield, and the horn of my salvation, my stronghold.*
> *3 I call upon the LORD, who is worthy to be praised,*
> *so I shall be saved from my enemies. (Ps. 18:0–3)*

Index

Belshazzar (son of Nebuchadnezzar), 133, 134
Ben Hur (Wallace, Lew), 76
Ben-Ammi (son/grandson of Lot), 103, 123
Benjamin (brother of Joseph), 87, 94
Bethlehem, 97, 98
Bible, *See also* specific Bibles, 1, 2, 6
    authors, 19
    citation standard, 2
    English translation, 17, 61
    history, 2, 6, 17, 19, 20, 24, 29
    importance, 137, 138
    original copy, 17
    overview, 2, 24
    selecting, 97
    translation, 2, 17, 61, 62
bird, 30, 58
Bishops' Bible (English Bible), 62
Blatner, David (author), 19
boils, 74
burning bush, 73
Burnt Offering (sacrifice), 79, 108

C

Caesar Augustus (Roman Emperor), 39
Cain (son of Adam and Eve), 24, 58
    God's favoritism, 58
    killing of Abel, 82, 99, 100
    mark, 134
    offering to God, 131, 133
    overview, 24
    punishment, 45, 50, 75, 102
    purpose of Flood, 29
    questioning by God, 32
    wife, 99
calendar, Israelite, 103, 106
Canaan (country), 93
    division by Joshua, 85
    location, 75
    Noah's curse, 58
Canaan (son of Ham), 60
canon, 16
canonization, 18
Cave of Machpelah (holy site), 100
child suffering, 24, 105
Christianity (religion)
    Abraham's impact, 24, 109

administrative issues, 128
    Ethiopia and Africa, 8
    fish symbol, 64, 106
    gifts for believers, 45
    Greek Bible, 17
    growth, 93
    importance of Jerusalem, 19, 28
    incorporation of gentiles, 85
    Law of Moses, 76, 79
    moral teaching from Paul, 27
    Pentecost, 18, 19, 23
    sabbath, 78
    sharing wealth in early church, 78
Chronicles (Hebrew Bible/Old Testament book), 23, 24, 26, 68, 117, 122, 137, 138
circumcision
    Israelites in Promised Land, 79
    overview, 24
citation standard, 2
commandments, 17, 25, 27, 67, 76, 77, 111
Communion (holy ritual), 18, 20, 79
Communism, 77, 139
concubine, 87, 104, 107
contemporary translation, 17, 123
Corruption, 89
Court of the Gentiles (area in Temple), 106
covenant, 99, 104
    Davidic, 107
    New, 2, 109
    Noahic, 58
    overview, 117
    Ten Commandments, 17, 25, 67, 76
Creation
    dominion over earth, 31
    God resting, 50
    humans, 29, 52, 54, 62
    Mesopotamian myth, 61
    order, 15
    overview, 2
Creation of Adam (painting; Michelangelo), 24
Cyrus the Great (king of Persia), 134

D

Dagon (Philistine god), 84
Damascus Road experience (life-changing event), 129
Daniel (Hebrew Bible/Old Testament book), 123
    additions, 25, 111
    Bel and the Dragon, 37
    Daniel in the lion's den, 12
    Daniel's Interpretation of dreams, 16, 29, 78, 122
    Daniel's visions, 122
    fall of Babylon, 123
    Nebuchadnezzar and the fiery furnace, 64, 133
    overview, 24
    setting, 70
    summary, 79
darkness plague, 74
date, 72, 83, 122, 123
Dathan (rebel leader), 133, 134
David (king of Israel)
    census of Israel, 27
    connection to Bethlehem, 99
    death, 83
    defeat of Goliath, 98, 99
    fall from power, 126
    God's punishment, 75, 102
    killing of Absalom, 107
    marriage, 110
    overview, 2, 117
    psalms, 123, 139
    Psalms, 137
    rise to power, 23, 25, 31, 59
Davidic Covenant, 107
Dead Sea Scrolls (biblical scrolls), 8
Deborah (judge), 86
Delilah (seducer of Samson), 87
Deuteronomy (Hebrew Bible/Old Testament book), 18, 80
Devil, *See* Satan, 45
disciples
    coming of the Holy Spirit, 97, 98
    definition, 29, 68
    description, 111
    fleeing after Jesus' arrest, 26
    speaking in tongues, 119
    washing of feet, 105

CPSIA information can be obtained
at www.ICGtesting.com
Printed in the USA
LVHW060456190919
631571LV00005B/57/P